ALL HEART

ALL HEART

THE JIM JEFFERIES STORY

JIM JEFFERIES WITH JIM MCLEAN

MAINSTREAM
PUBLISHING

EDINBURGH AND LONDON

First published in Great Britain in 1998 by
MAINSTREAM PUBLISHING COMPANY (EDINBURGH) LTD
7 Albany Street
Edinburgh EH1 3UG

ISBN 1 84018 152 4

A catalogue record for this book is available from the British Library

Typeset in Book Antiqua
Printed and bound in Great Britain by Butler & Tanner Ltd

CONTENTS

THE FAN

Saturday, 21 April 1956: Hearts 3 Celtic 1 - the day the Scottish Cup was won by arguably one of the finest Hearts teams of all time and the famous trophy was brought back to Edinburgh for the first time in 42 years.

I was only six years old at the time but I was soon to learn the significance of the occasion. After all, I came from a family who had always been Hearts supporters, and my mum, Helen, was a distant relation of the legendary Willie Bauld, a Tynecastle folk hero.

It was not long before I was immersed in the family tradition of following the Hearts, and when I started to take an active interest in the game at primary school I was often told and retold the stories of the great victory over Celtic, when more than 133,000 spectators crammed into Hampden Park, the triumphant return to Edinburgh and the open-top bus route of the packed streets. Little did I imagine that it would be 42 years before the famous trophy was back in the city and that I would be the manager to end the long, barren years with Hearts, who had been the butt of many jokes about always falling at the final hurdle.

It hurt as a supporter and as a player, and it was with great pride and an equal helping of humility that I held the famous trophy aloft as we toured the streets in May after the victory over Rangers at Celtic Park. Everywhere I looked the city was awash with maroon. The reception was incredible – one big happy family out on the streets of Edinburgh to celebrate the end of all those years of waiting.

However, it was not Jim Jefferies who had brought the Scottish Cup back to the capital city: it was the Hearts team of 1998. I am the leader of the team and, as anyone who knows anything about football will readily admit, success in this sport at any level is not just the work of one or two individuals – it is achieved through team effort first and foremost.

That family feeling, the warmth and the togetherness always strikes a chord with me when I hear the chants ring out of 'There's only one Jim Jefferies', for my father is quick to point out that he's Jim Jefferies. As ever, my jocular response is, 'Dad, you've always been known as Jimmy,' and then we would have a good laugh about it.

It is that strong family bond, the togetherness, which has always been so important to me, all coming from my upbringing in the mining village of Wallyford on the east side of Edinburgh, a traditional stronghold of Hearts supporters. Of course, when the community of Wallyford is mentioned the name that immediately springs to the minds of most footballing people is that of the late and great Jock Wallace, who was an immense figure in the Scottish game for many years. The Big Man achieved so much with Rangers, but he also had a major influence on the careers of so many players, one way or another. I am no exception as you will learn later on.

In fact, I first started playing my football on our own field of dreams in the village, the little swing park in the middle of the council estate where the Wallace family home overlooked the pitch and was located between my own parents' home and that of my grandparents. The Jefferies' family loyalty to Hearts probably stemmed from my grandfather on my mother's side, William Johnstone, and all the football talk in the house was centred around what was going on at Tynecastle. But in those early years all my interest was in getting out to that park and playing football.

It was a hard life in a close-knit community but a happy one. However, every family suffers their ups and downs and we had our sad moments as well, none more so than the loss of my eight-year-old sister Elaine. It was in the run-up to Christmas and Elaine was on her way home to get ready for the school party when she was involved in a road accident and was fatally injured. It was a terrible loss and particularly so for my mum because Elaine was the only daughter in the family. That was a tragic time and every year around Christmas my thoughts and, naturally, the same goes for the rest of the family, are with Elaine. It is something I will never get over.

Every Christmas the most prized presents of all were the Hearts strip, top, shorts and socks, the tracksuit and a new ball, and no matter the weather – even with snow on the ground – I was out there with my younger brother, Billy, with the new gear on playing football. In fact, the whole street was there, all ages, trying out their new clothes and playing those matches that seemed to last forever with the only breaks being for dinner and tea and then being chased in when darkness started to fall.

In those days, of course, football strips were solely for wearing when playing and not, as is the norm these days, being worn for almost any occasion – especially the tops.

I'll never forget the day I was taken to my first match at Tynecastle, for a very simple reason – I hardly saw a ball being kicked. When you are away from the village for as long as I have now been you do tend to forget the names of many people, but I will never forget Willie Reid.

Willie was a great Hearts man who lived quite close to us. He knew I was keen on the Hearts and took me up to Tynecastle for my first game – it was the old Edinburgh Select, a joint team made up of Hearts and Hibs players, and they played against Chelsea that time. These were games at the start of the season which attracted massive attendances. That was the time when there was no segregation, the supporters stood side by side, and I remember coming into the ground from the Wheatfield Road end and being hit by a wall of bodies. There was just nowhere to go and, being so wee, I could hardly see the pitch.

But it was a great experience, a dream come true for me to go to Tynecastle, and I caught the bug and was hooked on the Hearts. I tried to watch them whenever I could and was there at Hampden Park when the next trophy was won, the League Cup, in 1962, with big front-man Norrie Davidson scoring the winning goal against Kilmarnock.

That was a wonderful experience, enjoying the victory and getting back into Edinburgh for the parade through the streets by the team. That more than made up for what had happened the previous year: the club had reached the final and were beaten 3–1 by Rangers in a replay, after the first game ended 1–1 when John Cumming scored the Hearts goal from the penalty spot.

That gave me my first real insight into the feeling that goes with defeat in a cup final, something I endured later as a player back at the national stadium and suffered the same as a manager until the big breakthrough.

My Saturdays revolved around football, playing for the school in the morning and then going to the Hearts games in the afternoon with Musselburgh Hearts Supporters Club. I was the captain of Wallyford Primary, playing as an old-fashioned inside-right, and I travelled with a few school pals. I still keep in touch with one of them, John Blackley, who is still an ardent supporter to this day, and we do meet up from time to time. We travelled all round the country but the two grounds my parents did not allow me to go to were Ibrox and Parkhead. It was all because the crowds going there were so vast. The stadiums were so different then compared to nowadays, and Rangers and Celtic now have two of the biggest and best arenas anywhere in Europe for both watching and playing football.

In my younger days Hearts were *the* club, a team packed with so many great players, and I did manage to see a few of them play in the latter stages of their career, particularly the Terrible Trio of Alfie Conn, Willie Bauld and Jimmy Wardhaugh. Then there was the great John Cumming, the Iron Man of Football, who was the model for any up-and-coming player to follow. He was a Hearts man through and through, a great lover of the game who gave his all for the club. I was fortunate that John was still with the club when I eventually ended up there as a player, and I learned so much from him about being dedicated to the sport and giving your all, no matter the circumstances. He was such an inspirational figure.

In those early years I had no real heroes, but the player I did like was Davie Holt and, ironically, I followed him in eventually playing left-back for Hearts. Davie was a hard man, a great tackler who always tried to make good use of the ball. He was one of the unsung heroes of the time but the type of fully committed player every club needs. Then there was the skill and vision of the likes of Willie Hamilton as an inside-right. Youngsters always tend towards favouring the front-men, the strikers who get the goals, and the man for me was Willie Wallace. He was a really good player who scored bags of goals and I remember being very upset when he left to join Celtic.

Those were great times, grounds were packed for almost

every game. The banter of the supporters was fantastic and I was one of many Hearts fans who would go down to Easter Road to watch Hibs playing in European matches. It was all about the love of the game, watching some of the top players in action and hoping to pick up some tips and put them into practice when playing for the school or the boys' club. In those days no one bothered about Hearts fans going to watch Hibs and I am sure the same situation applied for supporters from other clubs coming to Tynecastle. That is the way it should be and it is sad that we are now in an era where segregation applies.

I was back at Hampden in 1968. I had just joined the club as a young apprentice player when we were back in the Scottish Cup final, only to lose 3–1 to Dunfermline Athletic. I had been training with the club for a while and we were favourites to lift the trophy again, but it just was not our day. It was another day of pain, but you have to learn from defeat just as I have had to do as a player and now as a manager. Nothing comes easily in life, particularly in competitive sport.

My dad was always behind me in everything I did and he was also a fierce critic, but always in the sense that I should do justice to myself. He was a miner who worked shifts at the pit and never had a great deal of time to take me to watch Hearts. In his spare time he played the trumpet in Moffat's band from Prestonpans.

There were no extras in life in those days – a big holiday for me and the family was a week at Butlin's in Ayr. Then there were the boys' club summer camps when we all went to Alva and lived under canvas for a week, I loved it. That sort of upbringing makes you appreciate things so much more. Everything we got was hard earned, even my parents finding money for me to go to the football. What we were given by my parents was treasured and looked after for they had worked so hard to give us what we needed.

However, actively supporting Hearts and going to games became more and more difficult when I started secondary school at Musselburgh Grammar. The focus was then on playing football more and more, and working on my own game started to take precedence over watching the Hearts. But it also had its good side, as it was at school that I first met up with Billy Brown. Billy and I played together in the school team and, eventually, paired up as a management team which has achieved what every Hearts fan wanted – a trophy back at Tynecastle.

THE PLAYER

The great love affair with Hearts might never have got beyond the stage of being a supporter but for one telephone call which changed my entire life. England was beckoning, the cases were almost packed: then that never-to-be-forgotten Friday night phone call during which I was told: 'You're going nowhere apart from Hearts.'

That's how close it was for me, but never to this day have I had any regrets about joining Hearts – even though nothing was won in my years as a player and as a captain. During a particularly traumatic period, I was minutes away from being the Hearts captain the day the players went on strike and refused to don the famous maroon jersey to play in a Scottish Cup tie.

It was all a bit of a roller-coaster ride for a lad who wanted nothing more than to play for the team he had supported since boyhood, who had stood on the terraces when they last won a trophy, and who so desperately wanted to win honours during his playing career. Playing football was in the blood and, like most youngsters, I was encouraged from an early age by my dad to play the game. He was a bit of a hard taskmaster, but the advice early on held me in good stead during my career and that has now been taken on into management.

It all stems from the simple philosophy – old hat, it might be looked upon by some – that it all comes from dedication to the sport, total commitment to the game both in training and playing, and always endeavouring to do justice to yourself and the team.

I played in, and captained, my school team, Wallyford Primary, before moving on to Musselburgh Grammar and, as I said, meeting up with Billy Brown, an association that exists today, and we have been in management together for around ten years in senior football.

Billy was well established in the school team long before me; I missed the trials and had to start at the very bottom and work my way into the top side at the school. Football was very much a way of life for me, as well as being a highly enjoyable pastime. At that time I was a prolific goal-scoring centre-forward, absolutely clinical in front of goal, and that led to my promotion through the various teams until I made it into the top side for the year. At that time we had Ally Brown, who ended up at West Bromwich Albion; Billy and Alex Martin, who also went south to join the ground staff at Hull City; with a few more who went on to sample life in the senior ranks.

It was all football, there was not much time in those days to support the Hearts, apart from going to midweek matches. There was a short spell with Wallyford Boys Club before I was invited to join Prestonpans YMCA, a juvenile side run by Bert Renton who was at Tynecastle, a matter of days after winning the Scottish Cup, to have his picture taken with the trophy. This made me the odd one out, for the natural progression from the school team was to join Musselburgh Windsor, a very strong juvenile side with a great record. My dad was from Prestonpans originally, a lot of the relations lived in the village, and that meant a lot for them.

We were not a bad team, but there is always one moment that can be the turning point for a kid; one that will put him on the way to realising his dream of playing football for a living as a full-time professional. For me that came from a big-match confrontation with Alfie Conn, the son of the great Alfie who was part of the Hearts Terrible Trio – one of which, Wardhaugh, went on to make a name for himself with Rangers and Celtic plus a spell with Spurs. But this was the big game in Edinburgh: Prestonpans v Tynecastle Athletic in a Scottish Cup tie at Holyrood Park.

Alfie, who came from Prestonpans, actually played for our team at an early age but he was enticed to go to Tynecastle – which were run by the famous duo of Dan Crawford and Charlie Woodward. Crawford and Woodward were also the Scottish scouts at the time for Sheffield United. It was in direct opposition to Alfie that I had one of my better games, as we defeated the Tynecastle lads by a handsome margin. Dan and Charlie certainly seemed to think I had a stormer for they had lined me up to go to England for trials with a view to signing for the Yorkshire club. It was a big step for me, and my family gave me their complete backing. No other senior club had shown any real interest as far as I knew. This was my big chance and I was ready to grasp it.

I was all ready to go down to England for a week's training and trials. The night before I was due to go, the phone rang in our house. I was told that the Hearts manager, John Harvey, had just appointed Dan and Charlie as heads of the scouting network at Tynecastle. Within minutes the phone rang again and it was Charlie, who explained to me what had happened.

I can't remember too much of the conversation but there is

one passage that will live with me forever. Charlie said: 'You're not going to Sheffield United – we're taking you to Hearts. How do you fancy that?'

I found it hard to take it all in, as everyone knew that I was a Hearts man and Hearts was the club I really wanted to play for. This was the moment I had been dreaming about for three or four years since I had become really involved in playing football. I was desperate for it to happen but, to be honest, I never ever thought it would. I was Charlie's and Dan's first signing and my dad was really pleased – after all, I remember him telling me, John Harvey was a Wallyford man, who lived in Musselburgh opposite the racecourse. His brother and my dad were great friends because they were both involved in pigeon racing.

I was 16 years old at the time and an apprentice motor mechanic at Musselburgh for the Co-operative. We looked after all the vans and in that garage were four or five fully time-served mechanics. My journeyman was a guy called Frank Duncan, who turned out to have a tremendous influence on my career.

Frank was a former goalkeeper with Motherwell and the understudy for a time to the great Hastie Weir, in an era when there were some marvellous footballers at Fir Park. He finished his playing career for Gala Fairydean and then went on to manage them in the East of Scotland league.

We had football in common and, incredibly, one of the previous apprentices at that same Fisherrow Co-op garage had been Jock Wallace. I think Frank actually followed Jock in the job soon afterwards and here was I following in their footsteps. It was all very uncanny. The Co-op connection continued with Greig Shepherd, who was a provisional signing for Rangers and went on to play for Norwich City.

I worked at the garage for 18 months, during which time Hearts farmed me out to Gorgie Hearts, who were a big juvenile team at that time. I trained on a Tuesday and a Thursday at Tynecastle and played for Gorgie Hearts at the weekend – and it was when playing for them, as a 17-year-old, that I broke my leg and, as all players do, went through a period of self-doubt and wondered if I would ever get back playing and make the grade at senior level. I was off work for about 15 weeks but the gaffers at the garage were very good to me. The were all football-minded people and allowed me time off to play with Gorgie Hearts.

I was so desperate to get back playing, I have to admit, that I did turn out a couple of times for Gala without anyone knowing about it to test out the leg. It was then that Frankie suggested to me that I should come to Gala to help me get back to fitness. The recovery went well and I was soon back playing with Gorgie Hearts and was about to be called up to Tynecastle. The system then was that you went straight into the Hearts third team, but Frankie felt it might help me if I went to Gala instead. He approached John Harvey about coming to Gala for a year (though still under contract with Hearts). I was happy about that and I had a fabulous year playing with the Borders team among professionals like Jimmy Peacock, Walter Carlyle (formerly of Dundee United), Ian Bogie and Alan Ainslie and a goalkeeper just released by Hearts called Gordon Miller. Gordon also had been John Brownlie's assistant at Cowdenbeath at the time when I had just taken over as boss of Berwick Rangers.

What a year it was – we won the Scottish Qualifying Cup and many other trophies. I also remember the games between Gala and Hawick – it was the Borders equivalent of Rangers v Celtic. At that time the Hawick manager was Willie McFarlane, who went on to manage Berwick, and in their team was one Terry Christie, who became boss at Meadowbank and who is now manager of Stenhousemuir. The rivalry between our clubs was intense.

I trained with Gala on a Tuesday night at the ground of Newtongrange Star, the same venue used by Berwick Rangers, who were managed by Jock Wallace, and Newtongrange, who were coached by John Hagart who, of course, went on to become manager of Hearts and has always been a close friend.

One night I walked in ready for training with Gala when I was met by Big Jock, who came at me with that staring look and barked: 'You're wi' me!' (An illustration of the Big Man's chilling attitude of always being right.)

I could not understand it and, to be honest, I did not know what to say. 'Am I?' was the eventual response I gave before I went in search of Frankie to ask him if I had to go training with Jock Wallace.

Frankie made it clear that I was a Hearts player and under his jurisdiction. I accepted that and got on with the job. But within minutes came the second confrontation as Wallace's giant frame appeared near our dressing-room door. 'Are you coming? Come on!' were his orders. I think I managed to tell him that I couldn't, trying as best I could to explain that I was told by the gaffer to get out there and train with Gala. Wallace repeated: 'Are you coming?' Getting no response from me, he turned and walked away without another word being said.

The first thing I did when I got home that night was to tell my dad what had happened and I tried to explain that Jock did not look too happy at all. My dad could not understand it either but it all became very clear early next morning – and it had me living in fear for a couple of days.

I was just about to get up and head off to work in the garage when my dad shouted up the stairs: 'Jim – you'd better come down here.' There he was at the kitchen table reading the paper. He said: 'Have you seen this? Big Jock is the new assistant manager of Hearts.' My first response was one of horror – I had to walk in there on Thursday night fearing the worst. It was a long journey that night up to Edinburgh. And I was only just through the door and there was Jock standing there. He knew me well from visiting his folk who lived in the same street as my parents. It almost seemed as though he was always keeping an eye on me, for there was never a time when he would not come over and speak to me and he was always interested in my career. He would always say to me, 'Keep off the bevvy.'

However, this was totally different and those opening words I will never forget: 'I've been waiting for you,' he growled. 'You'll be wi' me the night.' And it was a night I will never forget. He got me out on the track and worked me so hard. I have never been so shattered in my life. I could hardly get out of bed the next day to go to work. It was a message I will never forget. When Jock Wallace told you to do something, you went right out there and did it without asking any questions. He knew he was going to Hearts; I didn't and that was my trial. Jock always kept an eye on me; he came to watch me a couple of times with Gala and gave his stamp of approval to me being called up as a full timer at Tynecastle. He actually made the phone call to me to tell me I was being brought in and he invited me to go to Haddington that night where the team were playing in a five-a-side tournament. As a quick aside, this gives me the chance to clear up some errors in the record books which said I signed from Haddington. I never played for Haddington but it was there that I actually signed for Hearts.

I always got on great with Jock. He was very hard but always fair. I think I was his type of player and I was very sorry that he left for Rangers. In fact, Jock always kept an eye on me and I understand there was a genuine interest from Rangers in me, but just when they were watching me when I was playing in a match against St Johnstone, I damaged my ligaments, was out of the game for a while and I never heard any more about it. That injury put an end to that.

I will always remember training with the likes of Willie Hamilton, Donald Ford, Tommy Traynor, Eddie Thomson and, of course, working with John Cumming. It was a great start for me as they were great people to learn about the game from. There were so many good players at the club at that time, and the first choice for the position I played was internationalist Peter Oliver, who was a huge favourite with the Hearts fans. It took me a time to make the break through into the first team. I was on the fringes but always seemed to miss out.

I was in the running for a place in the squad for a summer tour of America, a really big adventure for any club to undertake at that time. I genuinely felt I had a chance, but I was left out at the last minute. That happened because a former team-mate of mine in juvenile football was John Cormack and Hearts were keen to sign him, so they offered him the trip to America to convince him to stake his career at Tynecastle. I was the one left out and it was a great disappointment as I was one of the young lads doing really well in the reserve team and getting a lot of good reviews in the local press. I felt I had earned a place on that tour.

But things changed and, eventually, my time came. John Cumming pulled me aside one Friday and told me he had told the gaffer, then Bobby Seath, who had John Hagart as his second-in-command – Jock Wallace having moved on to Rangers by now – that I was ready for it.

The first thing I did, after telling my dad, was to head for Wallyford Primary School on the way home to seek out Hugh Adams, the janitor. I had played for the school and had gone on to help out in the coaching and I had even refereed matches between the local schools.

The kids loved a Hearts player refereeing their game and I enjoyed it. I wanted to help the kids, for I have always felt that professionals should put something back into the game. Before I knew what was happening, the news was all round the school and I was in and out of classrooms, being hailed as the former pupil who was about to make his big debut for Hearts.

That first match with Hearts was a big day for me. Our opponents were East Fife, a really strong and powerful First-Division side in those days, and the match was played at Bayview. It did not start too well – we were 2–0 down – but we managed to equalise by the end of the match to earn a share of the points.

I was initially seen as someone who would win the ball in the middle of the park and was out of the side when John Hagart stepped into the managerial chair. Hearts had a lot of good experienced players at the club and it was a time of change. Davie Clunie and Jimmy Brown were established in the side, as was Donald Ford up front. Roy Kay and Harry Kinnear were two of the young lads who were pushed into the side. Eddie Thomson and Alan Anderson were in the defence and for a long time I played alongside big Alan, it was a good learning experience.

But it was at left-back that I established myself and, of course, I was part of that disastrous 7–0 defeat by Hibs. Defeats do not come any worse than that for a Hearts player anywhere, anytime. Hibs were a good side and I was playing in my first derby. I did not know I had even been chosen until very late on. I got my place because Ian Sneddon pulled out through injury. I will always remember we had two great chances to be first on the score-sheet, but Eric Carruthers and then Tommy Murray missed. But the rest is history: we were destroyed on the day and how it hurt.

I remember the next derby at Tynecastle, this time we got some kind of revenge with a 4-1 victory. By that time we had changed things around and played a 4-2-4 system with Kenny Aird wide on the right and Rab Prentice going down the left. There was a lot of skill in the side but we never managed to win anything.

There's no doubt in my mind that Bobby Seath was one of the best coaches I ever worked with. You always remember the boss who gives you your derby debut, but he was also a great guy to work with. His knowledge of the game was immense and, as a coach, he was a good as anyone else. He would have been welcomed at any club.

With John Hagart in charge we got to the Scottish Cup final in 1976 at Hampden, the final that will always be remembered for Derek Johnstone – the Rangers and Scotland star – scoring before three o'clock, the scheduled starting time, after the match started early. That was the result that earned Rangers the treble. It was a bit of a nightmare and before half-time Alex MacDonald, who went on to be an outstanding servant to Hearts both as a player and a manager, scored a second with a low shot through a ruck of players which gave Jim Cruickshank no chance at all.

It was my first final, an occasion never to be forgotten, especially as the drama began within the first seconds. Alex Miller had possession in the right-back area and Derek made the run to break down the right. I went with him and we both anticipated the pass, but we had to check when Alex knocked the ball to the inside and, as we both turned, we collided and referee Bobby Davidson from Airdrie gave a free-kick. In this situation my job was to pick up Derek in open play while John Gallacher was detailed to pick him up at set-pieces. Before we could get organised, Derek nipped between us and headed the ball into the back of the net.

But that appearance in the final earned us a place in the European Cup-Winners' Cup. Before our European campaign we headed off on a marvellous tour of the Far East and Australia. The tour would be the last for John Cumming as trainer. John was a wonderful servant to Hearts and a huge influence on my career. He seemed to take me under his wing; I was a similar type of honest, hard-grafting pro but, I am first to admit, I was never in the same class as the 'Iron Man'. There was no such thing as a friendly with him, be it a Cup final or a five-a-side in training. It was all about winning, and he respected players who went in to make the full-blooded tackles against him. He always gave 100 per cent. If there was any conflict between players he had his own way of sorting it out: he would take the 'offenders' up to the famous Brown Gymnasium in the main stand – it no longer exists these days – and would hand them a pair of boxing gloves. I was up there a few times myself, and it was mostly with John. I do not think I could say I was the winner from these confrontations.

John was a great man for training circuits and it was really tough work. Pre-season was hard going, and there was nothing worse than the runs up the Pentland Hills. We would be pounding out the miles, getting more and more tired by the minute. A gate to a field would be looming large but John was not for stopping to open it; over the top we went, doing a forward somersault on the way out. He was an incredible man who had the utmost respect of everyone on the playing staff at Tynecastle. John typified what being a winner is. He showed that during his playing career and, as a member of the staff, he was a tremendous driving force. He simply lived for Heart of Midlothian Football Club and it was sad the way he went. John was not paid a great deal of money and I do not think he was fully appreciated for all he had done for the club over the years and in so many capacities. He worked morning, noon and night and I am sure he would have been at Tynecastle until he was unable to carry on. I, for one, would have welcomed that, as he is the type of wholehearted, committed individual who would always have a role to play at any football club. It was a sad day when he departed the scene.

However, it shows the mark of the man that, having that done to him, he never ever came out in public to criticise the club. There were no sour grapes from him and, to this day, he still turns up at Tynecastle for home matches. He looks for no favours, but I never miss the chance to have a few words with him. He is a very unassuming character and there are times when I have to search him out to have these conversations. John Cumming is always worth listening to, and I regard him as one of the greatest Hearts men of all time.

With John no longer part of the scene, there were further changes at the club as we embarked on my first-ever European experience. In the Cup-Winners' Cup, our first tie was against Locomotiv Leipzig in East Germany. Getting there was an experience in itself: a flight to West Berlin and then spending hours at the famous Checkpoint Charlie surrounded by soldiers and having our passports checked time after time. As we sat about waiting, Rab Prentice turned to one of the lads and asked quite seriously: 'Which one of these guards is Charlie?' That released the tension as we set out on an horrendous five-hour bus journey into the heart of East Germany. This was a step into the unknown for all of us and we played quite well in the first leg, but I have to say we were fortunate to come away with only a 2–0 defeat. No one gave us much hope for the second leg back at Tynecastle, but it turned out to be one of the greatest European nights in the history of the club.

Leipzig actually scored early on to make the deficit 3–0 and I remember sitting on the bench – I had missed the previous couple of games because of a ligament injury – when we pulled one back. Early on in the game I turned to my mates and said to them that I still fancied our chances of scoring a few goals. Just before the interval John Gallacher picked up a knock and had to come off. I was on the pitch and it turned out to be the most fantastic 45 minutes of my career. We just went absolutely crazy, scoring five goals in the second half – a feat that was thought impossible in European football – no one could believe what was happening and the German side were absolutely stunned when Hearts started to dominate the match. Soon the goals were flying in for us and, in the end, we had pulled off an incredible 5–1 victory on the night and a 5–3 triumph over the two legs. Our defenders played their part, Roy Kay got on the scoresheet as did Jimmy Brown with a lucky goal. He maintains to this day he meant to score; but I am sure it was a cross that ended up in the back of the net. Willie Gibson, a great player for Hearts who scored an enormous number of goals, bagged a couple, with the hard-working Drew Busby also on target.

The next round was against Hamburg and we were back in Germany for the first leg. Although we lost 4–2 over there, we felt that the goals from Donald Park and Busby would give us a good chance in the return. This is perhaps the appropriate time to set the record straight about the much talked about game between Hearts and the press, which took place after a training session in Hamburg before the European tie. We actually gave the press Jim Cruickshank to play in goal to make their number up to around 50 against our 11 for the brief encounter. And no, it is not true that the game went on for ages until Hearts grabbed the equaliser. It was a bit of fun and I can confirm that Ken Robertson of the *Sunday Express* did nutmeg Roy Kay, which gave us all a good laugh.

It all went terribly wrong for us in the second leg at Tynecastle. Expectations were high, especially after the Leipzig result, that we would overcome the mighty Germans. It was not to be and we were completely annihilated on the night, losing 4–1 – 8–3 on aggregate. In fact, that European experience seemed to be a major turning-point in the club's fortunes. From then on, the club seemed to deteriorate rapidly; there were clear financial problems which were harming the club, and, things were not going as well as they should have. A lot of new players were brought in, on the playing side, but it was a big gamble to bring in players from a lower division. They were a great bunch of lads but, as time would prove, just not good enough to play at the higher level. It was downhill all the way after that – very depressing times for those who had a real feeling for Hearts.

The inevitable eventually happened: Hearts were relegated and, soon afterwards, that led to the appointment of Willie Ormond as manager. He had been the Scotland boss and did a terrific job for our country. He had his own particular style but no one could possibly criticise the job he did for the national team. It was his job to bring us back into the Premier League and that was a really tough season for us. We were the big club among the so-called lesser teams and the club everyone else wanted to topple. It is a very similar scenario to what faces Alex McLeish and Hibs in the 1998–99 season. It is going to be a hard haul for Hibs, but I want them back in the top league as fast as possible, as the domestic scene is not the same in Edinburgh without the traditional capital derbies. The city needs our two teams competing strongly at the highest level year after year. Football thrives on inter-city rivalry, and it's a special day – often with the best football of the season – for fans and players alike.

Willie, of course, was a famous Hibs player, a member of the Famous Five, and, it was a hard season for us, even though, he eventually managed to get us back up again, only for us to be relegated again a couple of years later.

Willie appointed me as team captain – the second time I had been given the skipper's role – and I enjoyed my spell working with him. Willie Ormond was a very good manager; if you look at his track record it is top class. He never said too much but he always seemed to have that sixth sense to step in to say his piece just when it was needed. He knew the game well and he worked us really hard in training. He went straight to the point, and was a very honest man and very approachable. Yet there was that aura about him which made you wary of him. That is always a good sign in a manager: to have that nagging doubt about how to take him. One thing is for sure, you could never dislike him. Indeed, I had one of the funniest experiences ever with him when I was captain. It was after a game against Ayr United, one which we desperately wanted to win. We gave the Ayrshire side a right roasting, dominated the game from start to finish but just could not get the ball in the back of the net. It was one of the most one-sided games I have taken part in, and I did not end up on the winning side. One of the directors at the time had come downstairs after the game and made a stupid comment in the heat of the moment, along the lines of: 'If players cannot put the ball in the back of an empty net from two or three yards out they should start thinking about looking for another job.' Of course, it was printed in the papers but I knew nothing about it at all until Malcolm Robertson came bursting through the dressing-room door on the Monday morning. He was blazing mad, as were the rest of the lads, and I was asked – as captain – to raise the matter with the manager. Off I went, knocked at the manager's door and entered with the back page of the newspaper in my hand. Willie knew what was coming as I told him that wee Malky was raging in the dressing-room.

The gaffer told me he had spoken to the director and had told him, rightly so, that any remarks made about the playing side should be left to the manager. We talked for a while about the issue and I will always remember his parting shot as I asked him what I should tell the players back in the dressing-room.

'Go back along there and have a wee word with Malky,' said Willie. 'Tell him not to believe everything he reads in the papers. I picked up the *Sunday Post* and read that Malky was man of the match on Saturday and I do not believe that.'

Everyone was waiting for my return and none more so than Malky, a lively character who was always chirping away about this and that. They were desperate to find out what had happened and when I passed on the gaffer's remarks the place was in uproar, lads rolling about on the floor laughing their heads off with the steam starting to come out of Malky's ears. That was the type of guy he was; Willie had an answer to everything.

Willie, with his Hibs connection, was not a popular choice among some as manager of Hearts, but earlier players like Willie Hamilton and Gordon Smith had played for both city clubs. However, it was not such a big issue in those days. I do think it is much more difficult in this era for players to adjust and be accepted when they make a move from one Edinburgh club to play for another. It did not bother me – I liked working with Willie. He was different and great company when relaxed. There was the memorable Hogmanay night when he took us up to the Braid Hills Hotel before the New Year derby. The game had little or no chance of going on because the weather was terrible, but we still had to prepare properly. At 12 o'clock everyone was summoned to bring in the New Year. Willie had had a few drinks and was in a relaxed mood. He had us up to around half-past one in the morning. The players did not have a drink; we were just frightened to leave. We were absolutely scared even to go to the toilet for we knew what was coming – an absolute verbal slaughtering from the gaffer. Frank Liddell made his move and the gaffer pounced: 'There he is, Mr Distribution, could not pass the parcel.' It was a bit of good fun and brought us all together. We all liked to play for Willie.

It was Willie who was in charge at the time of the infamous incident when all the players threatened to go on strike. It was the most incredible period for the Hearts and one that I would never want to go through again, particularly as I was captain at the time. It was a Scottish Cup tie at Dumbarton and it was the only game on that day as the country was in the grip of an Arctic freeze.

Dumbarton were desperate to play the tie as they knew the conditions would make it a great leveller and give them a marvellous chance of causing a big upset. The pitch was like the Sahara desert with ton upon ton of sand poured on top of the brick-hard surface. It was never going to be a game of football. But, during the last-minute build-up to the tie, there was a row about money. All the talk was about taking absolutely no chances at Boghead, hold out if it was necessary to take the tie back to Tynecastle for the replay. The priority was to overcome the Dumbarton side – even if it needed two attempts. A successful Scottish Cup run can generate a lot of money, and Hearts needed cash in these difficult times. That was fine, but the directors insisted that no money would be paid to the players for even getting a draw to keep us in the Cup. The players did not think it was at all right and would have even settled for half the bonus to take the tie back to Edinburgh. The directors would have none of it and then came the big problem.

Some of the players were really upset and what flashed through my mind at the time was that here was I, Jim Jefferies, as the captain who will go down in history as the skipper of Hearts when the players went out on strike. The few hours before the game were really tense and the players were really determined. Even before the pre-match meal the gaffer took us all aside and told us about the terrible repercussions that there would be if we did not go ahead and play in the Cup tie. But there was no giving in and, as we arrived at the ground around about two o'clock, the strike threat was very real. This was a time for decisiveness and I had made up my mind, no matter the strength of the argument, there was no way I was going on strike.

The dressing-room scene 45 minutes before the three o'clock kick-off time was incredible. There were only three players out of the entire squad who were prepared to play and who actually started to get ready for action. The rest of the lads were just sitting there, refusing to move. It was impossible for me but, as captain, I had to stand up for what I considered to be right, and I was strong in the belief that to strike was the wrong thing to do. I just could not do it; a vast following of Hearts supporters were on their way to the game and I could not let them down. I do not think we would have ever been forgiven by the fans, all of them, whether or not they made the trip to Boghead, for refusing to play for the club. We were all under contract and I had to tell the players they were doing the wrong thing. I tried to tell them about the repercussions, that no money would be coming in, as we would be in breach of our terms of contract. At the last minute I got them to realise it was wrong, the lads decided to play and avoided an enormous amount of hassle. Make no mistake about it, the players were right to complain bitterly about the lack of payment, but going on strike was not the answer. Getting out there and playing the game stopped a lot of heartache for us all. It should never have happened in the first place, but this confrontation really illustrated just how serious the problems were at Tynecastle at that time.

I hate to say it, but I have to be honest and say that Hearts were not a happy club or a good place to be. The money problems were starting to bite in a big way; cuts were being made all over the place and it did not take a genius to appreciate that the club was on the way down. We, in the dressing-room, of course, could do nothing about it, but for a man like myself who has a great love for Hearts it really hurt very badly. Changes were duly made: Willie left, soon after Archie Martin took over as chairman; Bobby Moncur came in with the job of picking up the pieces, but the rumbling continued in the back room as the boardroom strife continued with Wallace Mercer in the background and about to move in. This was when all the changes started to happen in a big way both on and off the park and, this being the time when I was nearing the end of my playing career, I became one of the victims in what was a very bad experience.

Bobby Moncur had brought up Tony Ford from England to be his coach and, while Tony was a nice fellow and all that, I could not see him being an answer to what was needed at the club in the time of change. For me, he did not have a good attitude as a coach. He knew a bit about the game, but had a terrible job in getting it over to the players. As an assistant manager, it is my view that you have to be quite close to the players, get the feel of what is going on in the dressing-room and be able to bring everyone together. Tony tried, but his attempts at being funny had that sarcastic ring and did not endear him to the players. He used to get some terrible stick from a lot of the lads who had been around the game for a long time and who were very streetwise. He just could not cope with it.

My departure came around the time Tony was eventually appointed manager and the arrival of Alex MacDonald from Rangers at the club. Tony was the boss and he did say to me, after the idea had been mooted earlier by Bobby Moncur, that I could have an input into the club on the coaching side.

During that period I was already involved in helping to coach the younger lads, and Bobby had wanted me to stay on to look after the reserve team. To be fair, Tony was not against that and, in fact, he actively encouraged it. The proposal was taken on board, but one of the directors scuppered the whole idea. That led to others coming in and, suddenly, it was all over for me at Hearts; I was finished with the club when only 32 years old.

I had walked in the door in 1966, had 16 years with the club, and I had been quite excited at the prospect of looking after the kids, even playing alongside them. Throughout my playing career I had been doing my own bit of coaching during my free time, and had helped out in the running of teams in my home village of Wallyford. I took a lot of enjoyment from that. I even remember managing to pick up an old strip from Hearts which was in the Ajax style. I persuaded my mother to pick out the threads of the Hearts badge and put one on which read Wallyford Miners Welfare Colts. This is how much it meant to me to make a contribution to encourage younger players to make their way in the game. The strips used to drown the under-12s but the kids loved it. We won a few cups and even John Hagart came along to present the team with one of their trophies.

I loved the involvement and had hoped to move into coaching . . . but I have to admit that I did leave Hearts with a bad taste in the mouth and it was all over the coaching job and a dispute about money. It was not pleasant at all, but I took it on the chin and do not hold any grudges. It did not dent my love of the club, no matter how sore it was for me at the time. One day, Bobby Moncur pulled me into his office to tell me that they were changing the loyalty bonus payments to the players. The old system was that if you had been with the club for five years you were paid £500 and it went up to £1,000 for seven years' service. I had received the second payment, when I was informed the system was being changed – £5,000 after seven and a half years and then £1,000 a year after that. That suited me but then came the bombshell: I was not to be part of the new structure because I had received that £1,000 a couple of weeks earlier.

It seemed logical and fair to me, after all the years of service to the club, that I was given the balance. But I was told that the line had been drawn and there was no way the club wanted to compromise in any shape or form. I was out of the side, went to Wallace Mercer about the matter, and he told me it had been Mr Naylor who had put the blockers on the compromise deal. Just before I eventually left I went to Mr Mercer to ask for the £1,000 payment after putting in another year, but he would not budge – he refused to give me a penny even though I had put in so many years of service to the club.

I had lost out on the £4,000 and now I was being denied a further £1,000. I was not asking for something I was not due, but he would have none of it. When I left he tried to say farewell to me but I just ignored the man and walked out the door. No sooner was I at home than Wallace phoned me and threatened to cancel my registration with Berwick Rangers, the club I had agreed to help out for a short time. He told me if my upset was all over £1,000 he would pay it out of his own pocket. Needless to say, I am still waiting for the cash!

I have spoken to Wallace since, for there is one thing about me, and I am confident every player will agree, I do not hold things against people for any length of time. I have my rows, I say what I think is right, but I do not bear grudges. I do not go over the top. But if that was the way Hearts wanted to operate and the way they wanted to work, I would never lower myself to that level. Bobby Moncur, to be fair, knew I had a point, but he could not get it through to the board. I was so annoyed after all the loyal service. I played for the club even with a broken shoulder to help out in a time of need when we were so short of players. No one could ever question my loyalty and support for the club and it was not a nice way to leave a place that had been my home, and a happy one for most of the time.

INTO MANAGEMENT

Football management is quite simple in the eyes of the supporter: if you have a winning team you are a hero and if you have a side struggling at the wrong end of the table you are a failure. Managers know only too well it is the end-product that counts, and how that is achieved is of no real consequence to the bulk of the fans who pay their money every week and follow their team here, there and everywhere. At the end of the day, all they are interested in is seeing the team they support win matches. Any manager stands or falls by his own record, but not all managers can be winners. Success in terms of trophies won is one thing, for that has to be equated with the resources and money that are available for any coach to put his own ideals into practice. There is no magic formula to management or any short-cuts to success, for it is all about a personal vision of putting a squad of players together and moulding them into a competent unit.

For me it all started during my playing days with Hearts, when I took time out from training to become involved in the coaching of local kids in my area, and I had the chance early on to bring together a group of youngsters from all the local primary schools to create a team. Once my playing career ended at Hearts I had several chances to go into coaching, but I did not take up the options . . . at least not straight away.

Like most footballers, I had not given any serious consideration about going into management and, as my career was drawing to a close, I became soured with the game after being denied the chance to do some coaching at Tynecastle. By this time I had set up home in Lauder, and I was on the point of taking over one of the local pubs. But, just at the point of taking up a change of direction in my career, I suddenly moved in another direction. It was the insurance industry that I was heading for, and it all came about through a chance meeting with former Hibs player Paul McGlinchey when we were together for a short time as players with Berwick Rangers. Within days of our discussion, I had a chat with one of his superiors and, in no time at all, I was off on a course to learn the ropes. I always give my all, no matter the challenge, and I went into this one full of enthusiasm and it all went very well. I became an associate of Abbey Life and soon established a thriving business in the Borders. I was not long in the job when the branch manager earmarked me as a possible manager and set me up to go on the necessary business course. However, when he moved on to a better position with Legal and General, he persuaded me to go with him. We built up a branch from nothing and we were so successful that we won a series of awards and bonuses, including trips abroad to the Caribbean and Vienna.

I had no real connection with football for two or three years and it was only through a pal of mine in Lauder, George Kerr, talking me into helping out the local juvenile team in the village that I picked up the bug again.

The local team had just escaped relegation but I was really struggling to find the time to take on the job, as I had just opened up a little insurance office in Lauder and business was going very well. My mate kept niggling away at me for weeks on end until I eventually gave in. It was an under-21 team, a bunch of local lads who just enjoyed playing football and it was there that I first met up with George Deans who played a big part in me moving, eventually, into the senior ranks at Berwick. That, however, was still some time away,

I made it plain to the lads straight away that if they were not prepared to show the same commitment to the team as me, then there was no point in going on. I am not interested in doing anything by half measures; it is all or nothing and in football, or any team sport for that matter, everyone has to be pulling together in the same direction. Okay, this was only for enjoyment, but that means that you have to work and give your all to the sport, seeking to do your best for yourself and the team. The lads did their bit and I took them from a season of just avoiding relegation to fourth in the league. The response from the lads was fine, everyone turned up for training. I was pretty hard on them but they were whipped into shape and I really got involved. It was a community thing and I remember the day when the players, the committee and myself cleared a snow-covered pitch to play a local game against Selkirk.

Then, right out of the blue, came a telephone call from Hawick Royal Albert asking me to coach them – even though my first season in charge at Lauder was still not over. Hawick were in trouble, ten games to go to get into the top ten to qualify for the new league set-up. They were in twelfth position and I went to Hawick to find out that they had just announced they had sacked the player-manager – a local lad who had half a dozen or so of his mates in the team and they had all walked out with him. What a start, half a team left and the deadline to sign new players was 24 hours away. The only people I could sign were amateurs, and in a matter of hours I went round a succession of amateur teams, including my own at Lauder, and had a new team ready for a really vital match against one of the top sides in Edinburgh. I remember it well, for one of the committee men from Gala Fairydean suddenly arrived at the game. He had heard about all the trouble at Hawick and wanted to see that first game against Civil Service Strollers at Muirhouse. Incredibly, we won the game 2–0, with two of the lads who had been brought in scoring the goals. It gave everyone a lift and in the remaining games we won eight, drew two and lost two – to the top two teams – to finish eighth in the league, and to book our place in the new structure. Funnily enough, as I was starting to build for the following year, we played Whitehill Welfare, a team which included a good friend of mine, Ninian Cassidy. Ninian knew all about my connection with Gala Fairydean, I played for them for a couple of months before retiring when Davie Wilkins was the manager. Davie was ready to retire at the end of the season and I was asked if I fancied the job.

I told them I already had a job at Hawick and was very happy there. One thing led to another and the phone call came to enquire why I had not applied for the job at Gala, a club reckoned by many to be the biggest in the East of Scotland League. I kept on emphasising that I had the job at Hawick. Eventually, I was asked to meet them and, with no ties at Hawick, I quickly agreed to take on the job and in the first year we won the South of Scotland Qualifying Cup only to lose in the first-round proper of the Scottish Cup – 4–2 to East Stirling. But we had more silverware in our own league, winning the East of Scotland Cup by beating Whitehill Welfare in the final at Easter Road. That put us into the City Cup and in the year Meadowbank almost reached the Premier League, we beat them at the Commonwealth Games stadium. That put us in the final against

40

Berwick and we beat them on a penalty shoot-out to become the first East of Scotland team in more than 20 years to win the City Cup. That was some achievement, three cups in the first season at Gala.

The new season was looming, the club dinner-dance was held in the Lauderdale Hotel which Wilson Young owned along with Hamish Deans, and they pulled me aside to tell me they wanted me to take charge of Berwick Rangers. They had just taken over at Shielfield Park and the offer made to me must be unprecedented. I was offered the job as manager and then told immediately they had no money to pay me.

The club was completely broke and had been in danger of going out of business. I took the job with no salary, accepting some form of payment for the number of points picked up in the season, and the way things had been going at the club, it must have been a fair bet that any money I did receive would not amount to very much. That was some start – and I did not even win a game for 12 weeks. It was just awful, but we set about playing games here, there and everywhere, looking for new players, for I knew a massive rebuilding job had to be done, and it had to be done for next to nothing. We picked players up from those games and I brought some from the East of Scotland after I sold what was considered to be the club's two best players – Hugh Douglas went to Cowdenbeath for £8,000 plus two players (Mark Leetion and Paul Cavanagh coming to us) and John Young was sold to Arbroath for £5,000 – money which was used to bring in more players. Suddenly, it took off. We were undefeated in 21 games, but we were so far adrift after that terrible start that we climbed only one spot up the table to move into second bottom place. The last team to beat us in the final game of the season were champions Albion Rovers, and we played them off the park only to lose 2–1.

It was at the start of that run that Billy Brown came to join me and, as everyone knows, the partnership is still going strong and we are now together at Tynecastle. At the time, Lindsay Muir, the former Hibs defender, was my assistant. We had played together a couple of years earlier at Berwick. Lindsay had left, but I asked him back to help me out as he knew first-hand about many of the problems at the club. I had no sooner taken the job than Billy, who had been doing well in coaching his local junior side, Musselburgh Athletic, telephoned me to wish me well. We had been great friends at school but we had gone our own separate ways, although we still kept in touch from time to time. He had initially phoned looking for a friendly game at Fisherrow and was willing to lend a hand if I needed him. I was finding it hard then because Lindsay was keen to keep on playing and I told him I was bringing Billy in, planning that the three of us work together. The time did come when things were changing. I had to drop Lindsay; he was not that happy about the arrangement and eventually moved to Tranent Juniors. Billy and I took on the training at the club and we set about rebuilding it.

One of the players who was there when I took over was John Hughes. He had been signed by my predecessor, Jimmy Thompson. At that time things were so bad at Berwick then that one of my first tasks was to go to Tranent with Wilson Young and George Deans and tell a 15-man committee at Newtongrange Star, where former Hibs player Lawrie Dunn was the manager, that we did not have the £1,500 to pay Hughes's transfer fee that had been previously agreed. We wanted them to take John back but they refused. We said we could give them a cheque but it was certain to bounce. It was a long night before it was eventually agreed that Newtongrange would settle for a first payment of £500 and would be given a percentage of any fee Berwick received if John was eventually transferred. It worked a treat for them: I sold John to Swansea City for £75,000 and I made them a right few bob before I finally moved on to Falkirk. For instance: Scott Sloan, a player I signed for £500, went to Newcastle for £45,000 and there were a few others who were transfered for big money – by Berwick standards – and all that helped to put the club back on its feet.

Credibility was achieved in the first season, and it was near the end of the season, the last game in fact, that my name was linked with Falkirk. I was still working part time for the club and I was set for a Caribbean cruise – one of my bonuses from my full-time job – and had to leave the game early against Arbroath, who were managed at the time by former Dundee United player Ian Gibson, and we gave them a 5–0 hammering. I emerged from the dressing-room at half-time ready to go and everyone thought there and then, because of all the rumours that there were flying around, that I was on my way to Brockville.

However, there had been no contact with Falkirk, but when I returned from holiday the approach came and the offer was to go full time for the first time. It was a huge decision for me, and for Billy, for he had a very good job with Ferranti. However, we decided to give it a go and what a challenge it turned out to be. Pressure is the most overused word in football, but I can tell you the strain was really on from the very second we walked through the front door at Brockville. Unknown to us, David Holmes, the former Rangers chief, who had been installed as chairman by Deans to give the set-up that local flavour – Holmes being a Falkirk Bairn – had told the supporters that he was about to make things happen in a big way at the club. He had gone round all the supporters clubs earlier and had told them that the club was going to win promotion that year. More than that, he boasted that they would do something that had never been achieved before: they would win the league championship. There was only one promotion place available that year and that made it some challenge to take on at my first attempt as a full-time manager. David decided very quickly that I was the man he wanted for the job, and all through he gave me his total backing. Just like at Berwick we had a really rough start, but when you move up the ladder it does get tougher in management. There was no love lost between Falkirk and Hearts and, of course, I was a former Jambo. Here was I, a former Hearts player, coming in and I was not a popular choice. The fans, I am sure, were expecting a big name – probably with a Rangers connection – someone like Terry Butcher or Graham Roberts. Here they had Jim Jefferies and it was difficult, particularly after losing five games on the trot. The day came when we sat down and talked about the whole set-up and David was very quiet when I told him that the players he had at the club would only achieve one thing, and that was to get the club relegated. His answer was short and sweet as he asked: 'What are you going to do about it?'

I laid out the game plan and he got up and told me to get on with it. I knew some of the most popular players with the fans had to go. There had been talk of Stewart Burgess going to Leeds United for £200,000, but I sold him to Kilmarnock for £85,000 plus I got a player for free, Stephen Cody, who was not even in the Killie first team. The fans were up in arms, raging at what had happened. But I had to raise the money to get players in.

Part of this major rebuilding job saw the arrival of Tommy McQueen and Simon Stainrod as part of the plan to revamp the entire set-up. I ended up buying in a whole new team. Some of the signings were not popular, but they all went on to do a fine job for the club. We had a huge job to do if we were to get back into the promotion race. A big turning-point was going up to Dundee to get a draw, we needed all the points we could get as coming up was a clash with Airdrie, who were flying at the time. The draw against Dundee gave me a belief that something was there and things fell into place at Broomfield when Sammy McGivern scored the finest hat-trick I have ever seen, and we romped to victory. In terms of football performances they don't come any better than that, and it was the launch pad for a superb 17-game undefeated run which took us into the top half of the league. During the season the rules were changed to award two promotion places and we were sure of one of them when we gave Ayr United a four-goal thumping. The title was now in our own hands; all we had to do was defeat Meadowbank Thistle in the final game. A draw would have been enough but we won 4–2 and, for Falkirk, the first-ever league championship was delivered. That was a great year, a fantastic year to look back on and we had the open-topped bus ride through the streets. We had been history-makers.

We went into the Premier League, stayed up, but the next year was a terrible time. We were crippled by injury problems all the way through and even though we had that incredible 6–0 victory over Hearts we were relegated in the second-last game of the season at Motherwell. We were shattered, so disappointed, but the fans gave us a standing ovation. It was unbelievable, they had loved the way Falkirk had played, for we had had some fabulous results during the season.

The lack of money caused major problems – local hero Kevin McAllister had to be sold to Hibs and Neil Duffy was moved on to Dundee, and we managed to get Jamie McGowan into the club in what was another demanding season for it went right down to the wire. Dunfermline were going so well, but we were given hope when the Fifers lost to Airdrie in the last game that was ever played at

Broomfield and we managed a three-goal victory over Hamilton, the very day that George Fulston had taken control of the club.

That made it a last-day decider and our entire season hinged on getting a result at Clydebank, with Kilbowie being one of the most difficult grounds to travel to in search of a result. It was the most tense I have ever felt in my life for we had to get a point. It was a hot day, the park was hard and very bumpy, and the Falkirk supporters were out in their thousands to give the players a fantastic reception. We just had to deliver and we got the start you dream of in these demanding circumstances: a goal after just six minutes. I have never felt such relief in my life. We had won the B&Q Cup, but what really mattered was winning promotion. Considering all the financial problems we faced, those were remarkable times and every credit goes to the players. To a man they all worked exceptionally hard and they thoroughly deserved the rewards.

The fans loved it, for they liked the way Falkirk played. People have always been surprised at my commitment to attacking football considering I was a defender throughout my senior playing career. But this is my way of playing the game and I will never change, no matter where I go in management.

There are far too many people in the Scottish game who try to make the game far too tactical and far too negative in their overall approach. There is this ever-increasing fear about losing and there is no doubt in my mind that it is hampering the progress of our game. I do not like getting beaten, but that should not be the overriding factor in the way in which the game is played. There is a basic need to defend well and I can understand the basis behind the negative thinking. Most look at Rangers and Celtic, see what they are spending on players, and get into the mode of concentrating solely on avoiding relegation. There's not much to choose between the other eight teams in the top league. A lot of managers talk about being positive and mounting a strong challenge to the big two in Glasgow, but then do the exact opposite when it comes to preparing their teams for the league campaign. They all look upon their first priority as avoiding relegation, for it is possible for any team outside the Old Firm to be relegated.

I take a different view from most on how the game should be played in Scotland. I am not saying I am right but I like to play the game my way, giving the fans a team that they know will be attractive to watch more often than not. This positive style, of course, does not guarantee that we will win every game. That is impossible, but at least we will be out there giving it a go and I think the fans know that.

I will not criticise any individual manager on the way they set out to play – that is not my concern. My first thoughts are always on doing what is right at the club which employs me, and so far it has not gone too badly.

I am not one of those managers who is actively involved in the coaching courses and who makes the trips down to Largs as part of the SFA set-up for coaching sessions and summer schools. It is not my way and that is that.

The only time I was urged to become involved with the Craig Brown set-up was when I was with Falkirk. Frank Coulston and Jim Fleeting, both members of the SFA technical department, came to Brockville to see me and Billy Brown. They questioned us as to why we did not come down and I had to be honest and say it usually coincided with us being on holiday during the summer or that we had other things to deal with during the course of a season. They were so keen to get the pair of us down there and I just wondered why. To be honest, I had been going along quite well at Falkirk and I did not see much need for me to become part of the Largs set and to have to listen to someone else trying to tell me how to do my job. I did get the impression that they were not too happy about my reluctance to take part. Maybe it was not looking too good for them that I was being quite successful at Falkirk at the time and showing that I could sort out a club, bring in players and take them to promotion . . . and that was being done without coming through the system.

The one time I did go to Largs I did enjoy the session – it was interesting, but that was that. I think there is nothing better than having been a professional player for a number of years and having learned from a succession of different managers. I have taken little bits from each of them, here and there, to expand my own knowledge, and then you have to do it for yourself, make judgements on players, wrestle with the cash limitations you have to operate under, and then see how new players you bring in fit into your overall pattern. It is all about hands-on learning and no coaching course can better that. Every manager I know will readily concede that there are times when you are swamped with advice from all quarters about how to deal with certain matters. But at the end of the day it comes down to your decision as manager. You have to be your own man. No team manager will get it right all the time; it will never happen. However, if you listen to advice, act on it, and it all goes terribly wrong, who do you blame? You cannot run back to the adviser and take it out on him. In football the buck stops with the manager. You always have to listen, no one has all the answers, but ultimately it is the manager who has to determine what he thinks is right and get on with it. If it goes wrong it is me that suffers. I never go around looking for scapegoats.

The big thing for me is that I have started at the bottom, I have been in the real world of football and worked my way up the ladder. I've been at Lauder; I've been at Gala; I've been at Berwick and I have learned through trial and error – and a lot of errors – about how to run a football club. I have made mistakes but every time you make one you learn from it and make sure it does not happen again. I will always do what I think is right, for it is very important to be your own man. I know there are some players who have gone straight into management at the highest level and it has not been easy for them.

I am not against the coaching schemes and all the SFA courses. They are fine by me, but what I think is, that it is not all about going down to Largs, getting a coaching certificate, that little bit of paper and badge, but never going on to be a success as a manager. I think there are plenty of them around. I have done the hardest part, I have shown I can do it both in terms of management and tactical awareness. I do not need a certificate to show that I can do my job as manager of a football team. There may be people with more qualifications who cannot do the job I am doing. I am not bothered about that. Football management is not about certificates; it is more to do with looking at what people have achieved with the clubs they have been with and then making judgements.

Don't get me wrong, I get on very well with people involved with the coaching system, including Craig Brown. He has done a truly remarkable job on the international front in taking Scotland to the World Cup finals in France after we missed out four years ago in America. Individuals do not come into it on the general issue of coaching, it is all down to personal choice and doing what you think is right to help you in your job.

I feel, first and foremost, my place is with the players. That is the priority and I have, in Billy Brown, a top-class coach who has been with me since those days at Berwick and who, like myself, is not involved in the Largs scene. There have been times I have been invited down to Largs but it meant giving up time working with my own players and I was not prepared to do that.

I have to confess that I was a little disappointed not to have been asked to be part of the set-up going to the World Cup finals in France. That would have been nice, the perfect end to the season for me after what had been achieved at Hearts. There was a suggestion at one time – I heard it when we were down at Kilmarnock – that all the Premier League managers were to be invited to join the Scotland set-up. I would have been more than willing to have made any possible contribution I could to assist the national team. After all, they are the flagship of our football and we all want the national team to do well.

I was never asked and that might be because I did not turn up at the last meeting at Largs. But, as I have stressed previously, the team had to come first and I was involved with them in the run-in to the end of the season and with the Scottish Cup final to play. I would have felt worse if every manager, except me, had gone but, at the end of the day, Craig took six. Craig, of course, has every right to pick who he wanted to be with him and good luck to him. It would have been a nice gesture to have been involved, considering we had done so well in the season and had finished it all off by winning the Scottish Cup.

I keep on using the word 'we' for what has been done at Hearts is a partnership, a team effort, and it all stems from the joint efforts of Billy Brown and me. People keep on asking us what is the secret formula behind our success over the last ten years. I do not think there is a secret, but if there is one, it stems from the fact we both know what we have together. We do not live in each other's pockets; we have our disputes but we are good for each other. It all comes from having a similar outlook in both how the game should be played and the type of players that are needed to bring the game plan to fruition. We discuss most things together: the training, who we should be going to watch. Billy now takes more training sessions than me, for the bigger the club you come to, the more demands there are on the manager. However, the team always comes first in my book and that approach will never change. Any successful partnership, in any walk of life, is based on trust and I know full well that when we discuss something about the training for the day Billy will see it is done. That is the way we work and it goes well. We are 100-per-cent men and Billy is very much his own man. That is the way it should be. We have total respect for each other and when things go right we both take the credit and we both take the blame when things go wrong, as it does from time to time. Everything we do is based on trust; he is closer to the players than me but that is the way it should be for the assistant manager.

I look upon myself as a hard but fair manager. I remember having Richard Cadete by the throat at half-time during the B&Q Cup final because he was not doing what I wanted. It had to be done and after the game he had a winner's medal in his hands. What had been said earlier was forgotten; the objective had been achieved. I've had my disputes with lots of players on the training ground but we never come away from that without the matter being sorted out and we are then able to get on with life. Running a football club is having everyone moving together in the same direction with the same goal in mind. That is what I always try to do and so far it has brought a fair measure of success – but in this game there is no time for standing still. Every week, every game, provides a fresh challenge and it is my job, and that of the coaching staff, to do our utmost to ensure that everyone is as best prepared as possible to give their all.

LEAVING BROCKVILLE

It started off like any other summer for a manager: putting together some new faces for the coming season and watching to see how it was all looking when the first warm-up matches started during a short tour of the Highlands. But the summer of 1995 reached boiling point for me, and it had little or nothing to do with the weather.

The season at Falkirk had finished really well. We had made a great effort to qualify for Europe and we missed out only in the last couple of games. But still, for Falkirk to finish fifth in the Premier League that season was an outstanding achievement for all concerned at Brockville.

That was it. We had all left on a high to have our summer break, never imagining for one minute what was to happen in the weeks ahead. It was to be the most incredible period of my life in football. I was immersed in planning ahead for the next season when all hell broke loose around me. I was on holiday in Majorca with some members of the Falkirk coaching staff when I first learned that Hearts had parted company with Tommy McLean and my name was immediately linked with the job, even though I knew nothing about it and there had been no approach made, as far as I knew, from anyone at Tynecastle. The speculation was intense by the time I arrived back in Scotland, but I simply got on with the job I was paid to do – that was preparing the team for the new season. There had been a lot of talk about a new contract for me at Falkirk but I still had to sit down and talk it through with the chairman, George Fulston.

It was on the weekend when I had agreed to take the team to participate in a small tournament up in Inverness that it all started to happen. However, everyone was talking about me and the Hearts job and I was taking quite a bit of stick from the players over the matter. We had the games in Inverness and then had a long-standing agreement to play a match in Wick, and it had always been agreed that Billy Brown would take the team up there while I returned to Brockville, travelling south in the car along with the chairman and George Miller. When we got back to Brockville I was taken straight into the boardroom and the talk centred around a new contract for me to stay at Falkirk. Unknown to me at that time, official contact had been made by Hearts with a call from Chris Robinson – then the chairman of Hearts – to the home of Mr Fulston. I do not know if George got the message when we were up north but nothing was said to me about any move from Tynecastle when we started to talk.

It was a couple of days later when I was first told about the approach and, without any doubt, I wanted to speak to them. After all, I was a Hearts man and I wanted to know what they had on offer and discover their long-term thoughts about the future of the club. That first meeting took place in the offices of Mr Robinson at Hopetoun House near South Queensferry, which was then the base for his catering firm, and we talked the whole thing over. Hearts had been struggling a bit for a few years and he was well aware that I had supported the club as a boy before I went on to play for them. He knew I had been watching the team over the last few months, when the occasion arose, and during this meeting the cards were laid on the table. We discussed what would be required and all through it was made clear to me that there was little money around to spend on new players. Chris and his partner, Leslie Deans, had bought the controlling interest from Wallace Mercer and were determined to get it right at Tynecastle, but they knew it could well be a long haul.

I made my position clear: if the job had to be done properly at Tynecastle we were not talking about one or two years to sort it out. We were looking at a five-year plan at the very least. It was all about bringing pride and credibility back into the club. They knew what had to be done and they wanted me to take the job.

I went back to Falkirk and had a chat with George, and he knew from the response of the Falkirk people that everything had to be done to keep me at Brockville. People will never understand what a manager goes through when he is in a position like this; I remember talking to Tommy Burns when he was first approached by Celtic after having done such a brilliant job at Kilmarnock and with advice coming to him from all sides. He thought long and hard about returning to Celtic Park, for he had done so much at Rugby Park, and the advice he reacted to and which he passed on to me was simply: 'If you go, make sure it is for the right reasons.'

The people with Falkirk pleaded with me to stay and I know if I had accepted the offer then I would have been the safest manager in British football for a good few years. I know there was talk at the time of me being offered a £1-million deal to stay, but the money talked about was never anything like that. George was desperate to satisfy the fans and keep me. Initially, he talked about a five-year deal and then it was upped to seven and a half years. The talk even got round to the building of a new stadium and the proceeds from the opening game coming to me. It was a really difficult period for me – the offer was there to return to the club I had supported from boyhood. It was a dream appointment for me, but then I had to look at all the problems Hearts were facing and compare them to what had been built up at Falkirk. I thought of all the hard work that had gone into the team and the superb response from the supporters who followed the team over the years – for they realised we were trying to play positive, attacking football. All the possibilities went through my head and what I found difficult was coping with all the advice coming my way from all sides. I listened to some more than others, but I knew deep down that I had to make the decision.

The one thing I have learned from all that turmoil is: when such major decisions have to be made involving so many people, it has to be done away from a football ground. I was really caught up in all the emotion of the thing when it all went terribly wrong that dreadful Saturday. I have never felt so pressurised, but I had arrived with my mind made up that I was going to Hearts.

I had told Chris Robinson of that decision on the Friday and that night I was back in my home village of Lauder and had gone out with a few friends for a quiet meal, just to get away from all the hassle of the previous couple of days. It had really worn me down and I was shattered – but there was still a lot worse to come. We were walking along the main street when this car came flying towards us. It was packed full of Hearts supporters from Gorebridge who had come down to the Borders to look for me and plead with me to come to Tynecastle. When they saw me they jumped out and literally fell on their knees in front of me, begging me to go to Hearts. 'You're the man to get it right: we need you back at Tynecastle,' they kept saying to me. It was an incredible incident one that I will never forget, and since then, I have met with some of those fans who are at Tynecastle every week supporting the team. What could I say? I couldn't tell them, for Falkirk had not known the decision, but I indicated that the friends who were with me might tell them that I would be the next Hearts manager. They got the message and roared off into the night singing the Hearts song and well pleased with what they had heard.

But, come Saturday morning, when I arrived at Brockville the place was besieged by supporters: mums, dads and young kids all pleading with me to stay. Billy already knew that I was going to Hearts and that I wanted to take him with me. He had packed the bags and was ready to leave as soon as I had officially given my decision to the directors. George quickly took me into the boardroom, looking for an answer. He had all his family there, or so it seemed, the directors were all standing around, and here was I on my own and they were all looking for me to tell them that I was staying at Falkirk.

They could not get started quickly enough, which was understandable, and, taking a deep breath, I told the chairman: 'I'm going to Hearts.' That was greeted with absolute silence from everyone in the room, then George started talking about all that had been done at Falkirk, the offer of the new deal and the plans for Falkirk at the new stadium on the outskirts of the town. He did everything to sell the club to me, used every emotional card in the book, and it got to me. He knew how I felt about Falkirk and the people there. I was vulnerable and he cashed in – big style. He just piled it on until I felt trapped in an impossible position. I had had day after day of talks and I had had enough. I felt trapped with no escape hatch. I know others would have just walked away but I could not and, suddenly, my mind was changed: I was staying at Brockville.

When I came out, Billy asked me what had happened and he was stunned when I told him we were staying. He could not believe it and before I could try to explain what had gone on, I was whisked away by the chairman and taken to face the fans and the television cameras. George made the most of the moment and was telling the people and the world that I was staying. After I had verified this, I spoke to a few journalists and I could not remember a single thing I had said. My mind had gone; I had to get away and all that was in my mind was to get home to the family as soon as I could.

They were as stunned as anyone when they heard it on the news that I was staying, for I had left the house a few hours earlier with my mind made up, the family behind me all the way, to leave Falkirk and move to Hearts. I was hardly through the front door when my wife, Linda, told me Chris Robinson was trying to get me. He was at a wedding and his mother-in-law had heard the news and had phoned Chris immediately.

Chris refused to accept my decision and I knew I had made a mistake. I agreed to meet with him on the Sunday night. I remember that day I had agreed to go to a golf outing, it was a long-standing commitment and I did not want to let people down. Golf is my other sporting love but that day was a total nightmare. I can't remember a thing; I was like a zombie. It was so bad that I was leaving clubs everywhere. My putter would be left lying by the side of the green, wedges on the lip of the bunkers, covers for my woods left on the ground. The people I was with spent the entire 18 holes running after me, picking up my clubs all the way round the course. I had gone completely.

After that it was the meeting with Chris and it did not take very long to sort it all out. I was joining Hearts and I knew all along that that was the right decision, in fact the only decision to make. It was just so unfortunate it had happened this way and that meant there were problems to overcome. Falkirk had made me a financial offer, but Chris was adamant that I would still be the manager of Hearts and really that was the place meant for me. There was never any doubt about that until that dreadful time at Falkirk on the Saturday. By the end of the night I was on my way to Tynecastle and there was no turning back. The next day I met George at the Royal Scot Hotel to tell him I was going to Hearts. It was a short meeting and, as you would expect, not a lot was said. George stormed off.

I suppose I can understand that George was doing his level best and taking whatever action he thought fit to keep me at the club, but it was really tough for me. He put me through the wringer. My one and only regret was that I upset the Falkirk people over my move to Tynecastle. I really felt for them – I know they had wanted me to stay so badly. We had achieved a lot together and their backing was tremendous all the way through. I had hurt them but I hope they appreciate the torment I faced at the time. I was caught in an emotional tug-of-war and it was the kind of experience I would wish on no one.

When I woke on the Sunday morning, after what had gone on less than 24 hours earlier, I was more determined than ever to go to Hearts. It came home to me very clearly that if I stayed I would be cheating the fans because there was every chance that my heart would not be in it. The Hearts job would have always been in the back of my mind and if Falkirk had hit a sticky patch, as does happen with every club at some time, the whole scenario of that summer would have been cast up at me. When it was all over it was a huge relief for me, a massive weight taken off my shoulders and it was later that week, once the dust had settled a bit, that I was officially named as the Hearts manager.

BACK AT HEARTS

My first day as the manager of Hearts was spent making the long car journey to see my team in action in a pre-season friendly against Derby County at the Baseball Ground. It did not take me long to realise there was a massive task ahead to revamp the club.

Breakfast was spent meeting the players for the first time and having a chat with Eamonn Bannon who was in charge of the side. I did not like what I saw in that first game – I knew there and then that this was not the way I wanted my Hearts team to play.

The big decision straight away was to change the system. Joe Jordan had first introduced the three at the back formation and that had been the pattern of the Hearts style for some considerable time. Everyone had become immersed in it, the young lads as well, and it was going to be difficult for everyone to move quickly into my style, which was always based on four at the back with options to change the strategy when the need arose.

I had been away from the club for 13 years and I was quickly aware of a strange atmosphere around the place, almost a feeling that there was some form of mystical jinx at the place; with an undercurrent that things were just not going to happen here. There seemed to be an acceptance that we were destined not to do anything about it.

The fabric of the club had changed significantly, with a massive refurbishment programme under way at the cost of several million pounds. Tynecastle was changing and changing fast. The first new stand, opposite the main stand, was already built and my first game was the glamour friendly against Newcastle United to open the new stand at the school end of the ground. It really excited me when I looked around the place, for there were real and genuine signs – in terms of the significant ground improvements – that here was a club on the move. For years nothing much had been done to the ground and now it was all happening when I was stepping into the manager's chair. It was a tremendous opportunity to really strive to put together a side that would fill this new-look ground week after week, for it would not be long before Tynecastle would become an all-seater stadium, generating a magnificent atmosphere when it was packed to capacity with more than 16,000 fans packed in.

The directors were at least making their moves to get it right. Chris Robinson and Leslie Deans had inherited massive debts when they moved in but they told me when I agreed to become manager that they had a five-year plan to take the club forward in a big way. They made it perfectly clear to me that it was thought necessary to channel as much cash as possible to rebuild the stadium for they were on a tight schedule to comply with the demands of the Taylor Report for all-seater arenas. Through no fault of their own, the improvement work was a bit behind schedule but they were determined to give the fans an arena to be proud of and, without question, when you look around Tynecastle now, they have delivered. There are plans, eventually, to replace the existing main stand – but money will probably dictate when that is done.

However, that is not in my domain – my job was solely to sort out the playing side and, because of the cash being spent on the ground, the team had been suffering. I knew this well in advance but, from previous experience, it was nothing new in itself to start a new challenge with not a lot of cash to play around with. There's never any point in moaning about it or using it as an excuse for lack of achievement. That is certainly not the Jim Jefferies way and never will be.

I knew very quickly that changes had to be made in the playing personnel if there was to be any hope of this club going forward. There were a lot of good players at the club, guys who had been good servants, but there comes a time when they should move on. I knew I would be upsetting a few players, some of them would be resentful, but I had no alternative. There was a situation where some of the players had been too close to the directors and I do not blame the players for that . . . but it was not for me and it had to be sorted out, as had a lot of things which I felt were fundamentally wrong.

Tough decisions had to be made, some people were not going to be happy and there were some players who should never have been allowed through the front door – they were the wrong type of player for Hearts. There had to be a massive change of personalities and I had to be strong to bring that about. There was also a core of players here who had been at the club for far too long. Situations had been allowed to develop within the club that were not right and that did not create a spirit of togetherness in the dressing-room. And yet, I had to try to get the best out of them in the opening few weeks of the season.

I knew the fans were looking for change . . . but I did not get this job because I was a Hearts supporter. Being passionate and being a Hearts fan is one thing; but I was brought here because I had had a successful track record at Berwick and Falkirk. Now I had to prove that I could do the same with a club without a great deal of money but playing at a much higher level, a club with a great tradition that had not been going anywhere for a good few years. Hearts Football Club only being involved in struggles for its very survival at the highest level is not good enough. It was not good enough for the club and the fans and certainly not good enough for me.

I had to change the situation around – even sort out the bonus system which really opened my eyes. Players were picking up good money after a sequence of matches when they were not even winning. That cannot be right – players have to be rewarded in the right way, that is for winning games.

Time was against me, I knew that from the first day, and the euphoria of my arrival – as is the case with every manager when he comes to a new club – quickly evaporated as we looked at the realities of the situation and set about trying to put our own plans into practice. Our start to the season was reasonable, nothing more, and the dreaded day was looming large when I would return to Brockville for the Falkirk v Hearts match. I knew people would turn up just to have a go at me, make it the most awkward 90 minutes you could possibly imagine. And boy, did I get pelters. It started from the moment I stepped off the team bus and it never stopped all afternoon. The game was incidental to so many Hearts fans, but Falkirk were desperate for a victory just to prove that I had made the wrong decision to leave Brockville. We lost the game that day but I learned a lot more than that. I sat the team down in the dressing-room, as the fans were still giving me pelters outside, and told the lot of them that I sensed they were losers: that when the chips were down there was no response, they wouldn't make things happen on the park.

From that day it would be different; there would be a new team out on the park. I told the players straight that in my view it was in a no-lose situation. If the changes did not work it would not really matter, for we would be no worse off. But at least I was trying to do something. It was perfectly clear that unless *something* was tried we would be plunging right back into the relegation area and I would be just the same as every other manager at the club over the last few years. I was not for one minute going to accept that so I set about changing things.

Some might not have liked it but I did not care a jot. This manager was for doing everything in his power to take the club forward and if I failed it would not be through the lack of effort. The players had had it far too easy for far too long; they did not appreciate how fortunate they were in getting all the luxuries that were going. Players and coaches at clubs who were doing better than us, and that included Falkirk, would have jumped at the chance to taste the treatment players enjoyed at Tynecastle. Whilst at Falkirk, my assistant Billy Brown ran about in a clapped-out banger of a car and the players had to club together to have hot food brought into the ground at lunchtime – the club stopped providing meals because the cooking was costing too much in electricity charges. That is the reality of life at some clubs, like Falkirk, and yet, here we were at Hearts being looked after so well, and we had just lost 2–0 to Falkirk. That was the end for me and the hunt for players started in a big way. I had brought Gilles Rousset over from France and he played at Falkirk as a trialist. I signed him immediately, for I saw enough in that one game to convince me he was the right man to have in goal for Hearts. The word was put out to my contacts in England and abroad that I needed players – and I wanted them urgently. Pasq-uale Bruno was the first outfield signing – he arrived on the

Friday, trained with the players that day and played on the Saturday.

It was also the time for the young players to come in and straight away I turned to Gary Locke, Paul Ritchie, Alan McManus and Allan Johnston. These were the four youngsters thrown in at the deep end. I remember telling them in the dressing-room that if this did not work I would try something else. There was certainly no going back to the bad old ways.

Soon after that Neil Pointon was brought in from Oldham, just to get change going, rumble the whole thing up and let people see what we were trying to do. I did not bother about those in the dressing-room for they had been given their chance and had failed to take it. Reputations counted for nothing in these circumstances and, I must say, to be fair, there was generally a positive reaction from the players to what we were trying to do. They quickly grasped that I was being serious, players either responded or they would be out. I knew I had to be ahead of the game all the time for, being a former player, I realised what could well happen in the dressing-room; I've witnessed the formation of cliques which, if not sorted out, can have a disruptive influence. The dressing-room has to be a place where everyone is pulling together, the place where team spirit is generated. I was the man who had to carry the can, even when we started to get a couple of results and things started to settle down a bit, there was always at the forefront of my mind the urgency to keep on changing things. Some players started to drift away, or were allowed to move to other clubs and, because of these departures, I was able to bring in Stevie Fulton from Falkirk, in an exchange deal involving David Hagen. I wanted to keep David but – because of the financial situation – the only way I could complete the transaction was to allow him to go. Stevie was important to me for what I wanted to achieve for the team. It all really stemmed from those initial changes and people realised that even without much money the club was starting to move. From the bottom of the league we went to the Scottish Cup final, finished fourth in the league and qualified for Europe. That was not bad going, and it really pleased Chris Robinson and Leslie Deans – for they had invested so much in the club and it was a really rough time for them, more than for me or anyone else.

What was really the major thing for me was seeing the young kids at Hearts coming to the fore and more than holding their own in the first team when given their chance. When I looked at this club the one encouraging feature was that, no matter how much the first team was toiling, there seemed to be plenty of youthful talent around. They had won the BP Youth Cup and that was due to Sandy Clark who, during his time with the club, did a quite superb job with the kids. He brought through some really good talent.

What bothered me, though, when I surveyed the situation, was that not many of them seemed to make the step into the first team to become established members of the senior squad. One or two made the odd appearance here and there, but that seemed to be the end of it. Young players need stimulation; if they are playing away in the reserve team, in their league, there is the distinct danger that they will become stale and face the danger of losing their enthusiasm for the game. If they are not good enough it is better they move on but, if the potential is there, the kids have to be given the chance to show what they can do at the higher level. That has always been my thinking and, at Tynecastle, it was long overdue that the younger players were given the chance. When I first brought the kids in, the response was magnificent and it seemed to send a surge of hope right through the entire club. They suddenly found there was hope for them and they would not be allowed to stagnate and, if they proved they had the ability, they would most certainly be given their chance in the first team. It was a different scene at Tynecastle – but there was the need to do a lot of ground work to re-establish self-confidence among my group of very good players. To be perfectly frank, the kids at Hearts were in need of complete rehabilitation to enable them to regain their confidence. Too many of them had been on a downer for far too long; their self-belief had taken a nasty jolt. They had been crucified by the previous management regimes, and we had to start working with them and show by our actions in management that we were with, and not against, them. We wanted to help them make their way in the game. They had already seen a few of their mates being given their chance in the first team and the incentive was there for them to reach for that same goal. The transformation in the place was incredible; the place started to buzz and it seemed to me that for the first time in a very long time the players were starting to enjoy coming to work.

This sparkle among the kids also made the more senior players realise that suddenly their places in the first team were under threat from these youngsters, and what really pleased me was the response from the more experienced players: they actually went out of their way to help and encourage the kids. But it went a lot deeper than that. The people who work so hard behind the scenes, both in coaching the kids and in the search to bring the best available to Tynecastle, were enjoying the spin-off as well. They were seeing their efforts rewarded and no praise can be too high for those people, the unsung heroes of football in many, many cases, who devote so much of their time to helping kids try to achieve their dreams in football. Every club has their band of loyal servants and they are invaluable at a time when we are all looking to unearth home-bred talent and take them through to the top. It is not easy, but we at Hearts are keen to give our kids all the help we can provide to make a career in the sport. Running a football club is not all about the first team, and the importance of youth development is an essential sector in what has been a rapid overhaul of the club. The emphasis has been very much on change, a complete rejuvenation and, even after what proved to be a fine finish to our first full season at Tynecastle, we never lost sight of the fact that there was much more to be done.

All through, my thinking about the rebuilding of Hearts was based on the continuation of my basic philosophy of putting out a team on the park that will entertain the fans.

There is nothing that excites me more in the game than to see a richly skilled, fast-moving winger taking on defenders, hitting the bye-line and delivering good crosses into the goalmouth. This probably stems from my early days at Tynecastle, from first watching and then playing alongside Johnny Hamilton, a real character of his era.

It was a great thing for me, early in my career when I was training with Hearts as a part-timer, when Johnny would come and work with youngsters. In the latter stages of his playing career he helped with the training for a while, and his love and enthusiasm for the game were there for all to see. He was a real character, a very brave, strong and direct player who loved to knock it past the full-back and then take him on for pace. It was the sort of play the fans loved then and I am sure they still do today but, alas, what was at one time part and parcel of the Scottish game – an out-and-out winger – is now in very short supply as we approach the millennium and that saddens me greatly. It's easy to conjure up the memory of Johnny, no teeth, bandy-legged with no one sure which way he was going to turn when he received the ball – and for most of the time I would doubt if he knew himself. But that was the joy of watching him, for he gave you that touch of the unexpected, the sort of play that thrills the fans. He was a fantastic character and in the game today, for all the progress that has been made and the money spent on big-name players, where are the characters that will get people out of their seats to cheer in appreciation of talent? This is what the game is all about. Billy Brown and I spoke about this very same subject when we first came together as a management team and, frankly, wingers are less hard work than any other player in the team as they are normally players with natural enthusiasm. These are the types who rarely need to be motivated by managers and coaches, while it can be hard work with others. Those who do not have that in-built enthusiasm often find it more difficult to deliver their best on a more consistent basis.

People look upon football as part of the entertainment industry and to meet those requirements we need personalities, not stereotyped robots who have a natural talent coached out of them. Allan Johnston and Neil McCann come into that personality category and, right from my entry into management at a senior level, I have always tried to play with a winger. At Shielfield we introduced Scott Sloan, a player who could either go through the middle or down the wing, getting past people and either finishing or delivering a cross into the box.

At Falkirk, I was able to bring Kevin McAllister back to Brockville from Chelsea, a local lad the fans loved for his infectious enthusiasm. He was one of the best signings I made during that happy time at Falkirk; others had tried in the past to bring him back to his local club but, unfortunately, the money was just not there. No matter the level of football, there will always be a place in my team for a winger. They excite me, and you only need to watch the response from the terraces to know that the fans love wide men as well. That is the way it should be.

Wingers will always be part of my game plan as long as I am in management, but they are becoming harder and harder to uncover and often clubs are now looking abroad to bring in personalities. Look at Rangers, they have signed an array of big-name stars over the last few years and there is no doubt in my mind that it is Brian Laudrup who has made the biggest impact. He can play a variety of roles and is often at his most dangerous when he picks up the ball in the wide areas and attacks defenders at pace. For such a tall man, his touch and movement are absolutely brilliant; as Hearts and other clubs found to their cost in his years at Ibrox before moving on to join Chelsea. The fact that he was voted Player of the Year in his first season at Rangers clearly illustrates the impact he has made. Laudrup, of course, is just one of an ever-increasing number of foreign players who are performing in the Scottish game at all levels and we at Tynecastle have certainly benefited from our acquisitions from Europe. At the time when I started the sweeping changes there came the Jean Marc Bosman ruling, the winning of a long-running court battle by the Belgian player to win the freedom of movement to play where he wanted once his initial contract had been completed. I don't think anyone could have anticipated just how much and how quickly that ruling has changed the transfer process all over Europe. We in Britain are now at the stage whereby a player comes out of contract when he is aged 24 and after that he can move to the club of his choice without any transfer fee being involved.

There is no doubt whatsoever that the Bosman ruling worked in my favour when I needed to change the Hearts team but had little or no money available to do the job of bringing in players of better quality. I never griped about that lack of cash, the picture was clearly painted to me when I accepted the job. Nevertheless, changes had to be made and they had to be done as quickly as possible. The easy way out for me would have been to sit back and tell the world that I had no cash and we had to get on with, and make the best of, what we had. That is not the Jefferies way. I had to make it happen, even with short-term deals, picking up free-transfer men from other clubs and bringing in player swaps just to freshen up the place. No manager gets it right all the time when it comes to signing players. I have made mistakes, I am the first to admit that, but on the whole I have done not too badly. Bosman certainly helped me in a major way to get things on the move at Tynecastle and it all stemmed from the arrival of Gilles Rousset. As the hunt started, a fax, one of many that come in these days from agents all over the world, landed on my desk telling me about the availability of this goalkeeper and he was my first really important signing. What a lot of people did not know at the time was that I had seven goalkeepers on the staff when I took over. Here was me, with not a lot of money to spend, having to go to the chairman and tell him I wanted to sign another keeper with so many already at the club. Among that seven were some very good kids, but this was no time to plunge them into the first team with the club sitting at the bottom of the Premier League, under a bit of pressure and going nowhere fast. Henry Smith had been the regular first-team keeper for years and had done a magnificent job for Hearts. However, he was coming to the end of his career at the very top level and I desperately needed a highly experienced replacement. Craig Nelson had been brought to the club by a previous manager as a potential first-team goalkeeper for the future, but things did not go too well for him. In fairness to the then chairman, Chris Robinson, he listened and gave me the go-ahead to bring Gilles over. Rousset's pedigree was impressive: 6ft 5ins, he had been in the French international squad more then 20 times and played in two big internationals, including making his debut against England at Wembley. He had performed at the top level in club football in France and here was the chance for me to bring him to Hearts without having to pay a transfer fee, thanks to the Bosman ruling.

He was coming to the latter stages of his career but, with goalkeepers, age is not that important so long as they can perform at the top level – just as Jim Leighton proved for Scotland in the World Cup finals in France this summer. When he walked through the door for the first time he had to duck to avoid banging his head and I had him on the training ground within half an hour on the Friday morning. Training was stopped as we set up a special practice match to see what he could do. I even asked our reserve team coach Paul Hegarty to play at the back for the kids, and I told him to make a few deliberate mistakes right in the danger area to see how the big man would react. I watched with Rousset's agent standing beside me and he quickly twigged what was happening. My theory is that the test of a really good goalkeeper is how he reacts when terrible mistakes are made in front of him, for instance, can he make the saves that can pull the team out of trouble? There are a lot of goalkeepers, technically very good, who simply do not have the ability to be the saviour. Of course, there is not a goalkeeper on this earth who does not make mistakes; but there is something really special about those who can often pull off the impossible when all appears lost. Gilles never made a mistake that morning and I decided there and then to put him in against Falkirk. It was a big decision but one that I have never regretted. Right after the game at Brockville he returned to France as he had a very good offer to play in Belgium, but I spoke to him at length about the long-term aims and ambitions I had for Hearts and managed to persuade him to come to Tynecastle. That sparked off a series of signings from abroad. Most of them worked but there were one or two failures along the way. I knew deep down, however, we were doing the right thing and the proof was in the performance of the team on the park. I just missed out on signing the top Norwegian player Egil Ostenstad. Scandinavia is a great area to find players and we had been watching Egil for some time playing with his club, Viking. We were very close to agreeing a deal for around £150,000, which would have been a magnificent piece of business. It looked all set up until my old pal Graeme Souness stepped in. As we know from his days at Rangers, Graeme is not frightened to spend cash to get in players and he emerged on the scene at the very last minute and took Ostenstad to Southampton for more than £600,000. It was very frustrating, I had spoken to the player and he wanted to come but it was not to be. He received a better offer, we could not compete and that was the end of the matter. That often happens to all managers in the search for new players. It is a hard business and not many people fully appreciate all that is involved, the work put in and the hours spent trying to sign new players.

Buying players easily does not happen in an era where agents have come to the fore and managers are almost weighed under by the number of faxes and letters arriving on their desks giving a list of their clients who are available either for transfer or on freedom of movement. Stephane Adam is another case in point. A contact from abroad got in touch with me and that started me making a whole series of enquiries before any decision was made to go and see him play. What helped us greatly was that Stephane was already coming to Scotland to train on the quiet with Hibs, and so we made plans for one of our scouts to have a sneak preview when he played a trial match in their reserve team.

Unfortunately, Hibs could not come up with the cash for Stephane, who at that time was still under contract with Metz. I sat back and waited, for we could not afford the asking price of more than £200,000 either. Metz wanted to keep him, but he was not getting a regular game with the French club. His contract was up at the end of the season and we decided to bide our time and invited him to our pre-season training when he became a free agent. His countryman Gilles helped to persuade him to join us in Scotland and we quickly agreed a deal, just as we did with Stefano Salvatori who was recommended to us by Pasquale Bruno.

All players coming from another country need time to settle into living in a new environment and get used to the demands and the style of the Scottish game, but Stefano gave us something this club has been crying out for for a very long time: a very strong midfield player who could get about people quickly in the key midfield area and be able to use the ball simply and effectively. It is all about balance when building a team and Stefano provided an important ingredient in the recipe for putting together a good team unit. Initially, Stefano was signed on a short-term contract but we moved quite quickly to persuade him to agree a long-term deal which has worked out very well so far.

Bosman has been a great avenue for us. There are a lot of good players available in Europe but the key to it all is choosing the right one. We can watch hundreds of players but, at the end of the day, it all comes down to judgement on securing the one that is right for you. Fortunately, our assessments on players have stood us in good stead over the years. We certainly have reaped the benefits of our activities on the continent. There are no boundaries in football any more. The Bosman decision has made it a very difficult time for football in general, but I am sure it will settle down and be good for the game overall. However, it has forced managers into a new way of thinking and has brought about a fresh challenge. Those players with good ability are most definitely going to reap the benefits and be able to retire with a lot of money in the bank.

The days of players signing long-term, five- or six-year contracts have all but gone and that has been accepted as a fact of football life in the 1990s. Some might not like it but that is the way it is and it will make life a lot harder for managers looking for ongoing success and being able to compete genuinely for honours. Given the new circumstances, it is understandable for players to look at moving around all the time, a couple of years here, a couple of years there and so on. The only way you have any chance of keeping them for a longer period of time is to offer them mega contracts and, in most cases in Scottish football, that is just not possible or financially viable. Some of them, the top players, have the opportunity to make a fortune in a very short period of time . . . and good luck to them. If the money is offered it would be madness not to accept.

Like all managers, however, I am deeply concerned about the way things are going, especially when it comes to the younger players, those who the club have recruited early on, spent a lot of time and money on them in endeavouring to enhance their careers, only to face the fact of losing them when they become 24 years old and are able to move clubs under the terms of freedom of contract. It means that managers looking to build a team through the progression of younger players through the ranks will be denied that opportunity. Agents are not at all interested in managers trying to build a team. They have players on their books and only want to get the maximum return for them by moving them around from club to club, always seeking a better deal with every move. What we are facing at Hearts, as is the case with a lot of other clubs in Scotland, is that we are in danger of losing a lot of our top-bracket youngsters for no transfer fee. They can wait until they are 24 and move for nothing. No club is isolated in this, and it is certainly not the case of me moaning that Hearts are in danger of being hard done. I look upon Hearts, one of the bigger clubs in Scotland, who, hopefully, are now fast building the reputation of being able to attract top players and encourage the younger ones to join us. I do believe, and in no way being disrespectful to others, that we are probably better placed to lure top players to Tynecastle from other clubs, once they are available under freedom of contract. This is due to the new-found status of the club, our recent success and the fact that we have already attracted several top-class signings.

I do feel that we are approaching a massive change in approach to player management. Team managers will start to sit down, look at their playing staff, and see when the younger players are about to go out of contract and become free agents.

If the early indications are that the player is thinking about moving on, then the temptation is there to move him on. This has been going on on the continent for some time and now it is about to happen in Britain. A manager is going to be judged now not only on his coaching abilities but his astuteness in dealing with the Bosman situation. With no money coming in through transfer fees, decisions have to be made much earlier about replacements, managers also have to have the ability to bring someone else in, and know where and for how much to sell the player whose contract is about to expire in a year's time. There has to be a general acceptance that this is about to happen, particularly by the fans who do not want to see their favourites leave the club. We can try all we can but if there is more money on offer elsewhere the likelihood is that the player will go. Brian

Laudrup is the perfect example of this. It is the general consensus that he was not as effective in his last season at Rangers when all the talk was going on about him moving away and his eventual decision to go to Stamford Bridge. I think Brian is a marvellous player and I would never accuse any player of not giving his all. However, we are all human beings, and it is possible that deep down in his subconscious all the talk of him leaving Rangers did have a bearing to some degree on his performance on the field. You do not get the best out of any player unless he is totally focused and committed 100 per cent to his club. In my mind, this will force managers to a fresh assessment; yes, make a player the best possible offer to stay, but if there is any doubt then he has to go. If a player does not want to play for you there is absolutely no point in keeping him at the club. It is not easy but, nevertheless, it will have to be done. My job as manager is to ensure that the team does not suffer in the long term. There has been a massive turnover in players at Tynecastle since my arrival and that will continue to happen in the future because of the changing circumstances. No one likes to lose good players and we have a real problem at Hearts for we have so many good players. Much as I hate to say it, we will lose out somewhere along the line and, in particular, to the big clubs in England who can give these players three or even four times as much as I can. There is no way this club could possibly afford to pay players sums like £7,000 or £8,000 a week in basic wages. There is no point in kidding anyone on; it cannot be done. We would go out of business very quickly. There has to be some form of equality over paying players and it can only lead to trouble and dressing-room discontent when one player is earning substantially more than the others. Clubs have to raise their level of wages to keep their better players, otherwise no one will be able to hold on to their most prized assets. It works the other way as well, for if a club is spending the money they once put aside for transfer fees or wages it will make it all the more difficult for a potential buyer to entice that player away.

To keep on seeking improvement at Hearts, and that has to be the objective, you have to move to a different quality of player and the natural follow-on from that is the necessity to move to a different level of income. Players might be valued at £1 million on the transfer market and, not being the daft bunch of individuals that most seem to think they are, will quickly realise that if they are signing for a club for nothing, they will want a big slice of that initial transfer valuation. They could be looking for contracts worth around £500,000 for a couple of years and quickly point to the fact that they are saving the club another £500,000 with there being no fee involved. That is the way it is going. There is every likelihood that, in the early stages of this new era, clubs will pay out big money in wages for four or five players but then find they cannot afford to go on like this. Whether we like it or not, football is business and clubs have to live within their means. All this further emphasises the need to remain successful; that is the key factor. A team playing well brings in the fans, generates money at the turnstiles, but, just as importantly, it is the corporate side of the business which can bring in big money from companies who want to be seen to be involved with something that is going well and is successful. We must never lose sight of the fact that all income stems from the success of a football team. No one is going to invest in a football team that is toiling. Just look at Hearts three years ago, struggling even to survive in the Premier League year after year, never mind winning a trophy. There were little more than 3,000 season-ticket-holders and there was overall gloom and doom as people became disillusioned with the club.

It is a very delicate balancing act to have a successful

football team and there will always be a downside to transfer dealings as happened to me very quickly at Tynecastle.

Allan Johnston was in a group of four or five lads I had
turned to after a few months in the job to show what they
could do in the first team, and I made all of them the same
offer over a new contract. I was very anxious to keep Allan,
and his departure is one of the biggest regrets I have about
Bosman. I made him the best possible offer to stay but it
did become very evident that the longer the talks went on
with him and his agent the more he made up his mind to
go. Possibly asking for higher wages was a bit of a
smokescreen to his overall view. We could not meet his
demands and that led to his departure – to the French club,
Rennes. Allan is a very special talent, the type of player
who can win a game with a flash of individual brilliance,
and it is my view that if he had stayed with us he could
well have pushed us even closer to winning the league.
Neil McCann can do that with his great turn of pace, and
having Neil and Allan together would have given us a very
important option. Allan was the first one we lost and it still
hurts me a bit. We did get £100,000 when he returned to
Britain from France, after he was unable to settle, to sign
for Sunderland. Yet, that was a meagre financial reward for
such a great talent. At the end of the day, however, the
bigger clubs, those with ambition and desire, will probably
benefit most from Bosman. Rangers and Celtic cannot sign
all the players. We at Hearts have to make sure that we
attract our fair share of the top talent. We cannot meet the
wages paid by the big two in Glasgow – they have bigger
resources, pulling in 50,000 for every home game while a
packed Tynecastle can only cater for around 18,000. That is
a huge difference in terms of supporter-pulling power and
the same goes on the corporate side as well. Yet we are still
a major club who will strive to continue to make progress

and give our supporters the best-available talent to watch week in, week out.

However, Bosman alone will not determine how Hearts fare in the year ahead. There is a vitally important balance to be struck in the recruitment of players from abroad and the rearing of home-bred Scottish talent. It would seem that we are not far away from seeing a leading club like Rangers having a first team without a single Scot in the line-up. That is the way they are going, the market place they are dealing in, but it will never happen at Tynecastle. Football in this country is very different to that on the mainland of Europe – both on and off the park. Our fans want to see good football, or course they do, but we must never lose sight of the need for the traditional commitment which is part and parcel of our game. The fans like to see the passion, the action in and around the penalty box. I don't disagree with that, but there is a need for equal importance to be attached to the quality of our play, not just thumping the ball from one end of the park to the other and then looking to score off little knock-downs.

We will always look to Scotland to bring the best available to Tynecastle – and we have done that already in our first three years – and we have succeeded fairly well in striking that right balance between imported and local talent. That is the way we intend to go forward, with the onus always on giving the Hearts fans a good team to come to watch.

DAVID WEIR

T here can be no greater pinnacle for any professional footballer than to play for his country and then go on to take the greatest stage of all – the World Cup finals. This summer Craig Brown took the national team to France '98, coming through a very difficult and demanding qualifying campaign to reach the last 32. In the process he carved his own little niche in the history of the game by becoming the first Scotland team manager to take the international side from participating in the finals of the European Championship in England in 1996 then reaching the World Cup finals in 1998. Eight times we have been to the World Cup finals, yet we have still to get through the first phase and that was an obvious disappointment to us all in Scottish football – no one more so than Craig Brown and his squad of players.

We were all proud, and pleased, that we at Hearts had one player who made the squad and played in the games against Norway and Morocco. The rise of David Weir from nowhere to international level is one of the most remarkable sporting achievements of this decade. Here we have a young man who wrote a letter begging for a trial with a senior team and then who, just a few years later, stepped onto the international stage and did not look out of place one little bit. I was the manager who gave David his chance and no one was more delighted than me when he won his first international honour soon after joining Hearts and later went on to France.

It maintains a Hearts tradition for, in the World Cup finals in Italy in 1990 – we did not qualify for the event in America in 1994 – we had both Craig Levein and David McPherson as part of Andy Roxburgh's squad. The breakthrough of David Weir goes back to the days when I was manager of Falkirk and was setting about the rebuilding at Brockville and, like every team manager, many letters came recommending players. Now, we all like to think that we check out all the suggestions that come our way and that is the way it happened for me.

It was in the summer of 1992 that a letter arrived from David asking for a trial. It is difficult to explain, but the more I read the letter the more I started to get vibes about the lad and set about making enquiries. He had just returned from America to his home town of Falkirk – he had been on a university scholarship – and was looking to play football. The first port of call was our local scout, Bill Parker, a school teacher, who quickly recalled that David had been with Celtic Boys Club before he went to the States. Bill spoke highly of the lad and we quickly decided to have him in at Brockville for a trial period. It was right at the start of our pre-season training, we had nothing to lose, and when I phoned him at his home David jumped at the chance to come along to the ground. I told him no judgements would be made early on: the first ten days were all about fitness and getting everyone in the right shape before the practice matches started. He could not wait to get into the training and from the first time I set eyes on him he most certainly looked the part, a big strong lad with great athletic ability.

He seemed to thri .: on the early grind, found it hard-going at times, b· ˙ wa⌐ always right up there. We started our first training session with the ball at the BP sports ground at Grangemouth and there was the usual cheering from the lads when we started. From the minute I first saw him on the ball I called Billy Brown over and told him to keep an eye on him. Our assessment was similar – we had discovered a special talent and signed him that very day. He accepted a year's contract and, for a guy who had hardly played competitive football for four years, he started to make great strides and – after just six reserve-team games – he was close to playing in the Premier League.

We had suffered a terrible start, nothing but a succession of injuries, and suddenly I found myself without an experienced centre-back. I knew I had to buy an experienced centre-half from somewhere and managed to recruit Joe McLaughlin from Chelsea, only for him to join the casualty list. I couldn't go out and buy another player and that was when I turned to David and told him he was playing against Dundee United at Tannadice, which is never an easy place to pick up points.

His opponent that afternoon was none other than Duncan Ferguson, the exciting big striker everyone was raving about (he went to Rangers not long afterwards for £4 million and moved on to Everton for another £4 million and is now the team captain at Goodison). David never gave him a kick of the ball; he was quite magnificent, just a different class. He is the one player in all the time I have been in management that I have never dropped. He has been a model of consistency who has gone on to play at the highest level. The only time he is out of the side is when he's injured and he has great powers of recovery – as was proved this season when he came back from his leg damage. When he had the operation – to correct a shin-bone problem – he was expected to be out for a couple of months but returned to the side within a fortnight and was like a new player – and an even better one.

Over the years a few clubs have shown an interest in signing David, but no one ever made a concrete bid . . . and that includes Rangers. I did speak with Walter Smith on a couple of occasions about David but it never did go any further than that, contrary to what was said and written in the media at the time. Figures were spoken about but I never saw any written offer. It seems that Rangers are a bit wary over buying players from lower clubs in Scotland, but that is their business and nothing to do with me. All that bothered me was that I still had the player at Falkirk and that pleased me greatly. I did tell Walter during our talks that I rated David as a future Scotland player and he seemed to take that on board. Talking with such esteem for the player was no sales gimmick on my part; I was simply telling it as I saw it. Of all the players I have worked with there has been none better than David Weir. He is a joy to work with, he always listens and readily accepts what role I have asked him to perform, be it at right-back, the middle of the defence or even in midfield, where he has done well from time to time. However, like all of us, he had his problems and things did not go well for him at Brockville for a while after I left to take over at Tynecastle. He did not seem happy with life and a few people, Falkirk supporters especially, kept on telling me he was having a bad time of it. They said it was like watching a different player, he appeared to have lost much of his confidence and self-belief. David never says very much but he is the type who needs the right kind of handling.

David is one of those players who always likes a challenge, just as he did when I first took him to Falkirk, he was desperate to show he could play in senior football and that is why he has achieved so much with Hearts and has gone on from that to be part of the Scotland set-up. There's nothing fancy about this player, he is content with being a team player, part of the set-up and not the main man. He's always had very experienced professionals around him, like John Hughes at Falkirk, the centre-back who went on to play for Celtic and is now captain of Hibs. When he arrived at Hearts we had Craig Levein and Davie McPherson, both Scottish international players, and he fitted in well with them, always willing to listen and take on board advice whether it be from me, Billy Brown or other players. A lot of his problems in the latter stages at Brockville is that he suddenly found himself as the big fish and that did not suit him. The time had come when he needed to get away from Falkirk to further his career, when I was about to step in he was actively considering a move to the continent. David was one of my first signing targets, but again money was the problem as we talked with his agent, Bill McMurdo, and our own chairman. As things often happen in football, the situation changed and David became available, a deal being struck that he came to Tynecastle in exchange for David Hagen and Craig Nelson. The actual money that changed hands was £180,000 and that has to be regarded as a great bit of business for Hearts. We had Scottish competition for his signature from Hibs, where Alex Miller was the manager at the time. However, the clinching factor was our association at Falkirk. Of course, every signing attracts criticism and there were those who questioned the need for a centre-half when we had international players in our ranks. It was just the fresh challenge David needed, out there to win over the doubters. I knew right away this was an international player, just as I had told Walter Smith when he considered taking him to Ibrox. This game of ours is all about opinions, no one is correct all the time, but I reckon I am not too bad a judge of a player. This lad has everything going for him, he has good pace, is good in the air and can grab a goal or two for you and, what is so essential in the game, he reads it well. Mental awareness is so critical in today's game when it is played at such a fast pace. He is a thoroughly good professional and his adaptability makes him such an important player.

Nothing would please me more than to have him with me at Hearts for the rest of his career, and if I was ever to be the Scotland manager he would never be out of my team. Mind you, the quality of the ball he supplied for Craig Burley to score the equaliser against Norway might have surprised some, but definitely not anyone at Tynecastle. He does that often in games as our front players will readily concede. Little wonder that his team-mates call him 'Hoss'. He is such a strong lad and is now starting to show the hardness and aggression that is so important for a defender.

The signing of Weir was all part of the overall plan to take this club in a different direction and getting them into the Jim Jefferies way of playing. Since my arrival, much has been made about the signings from abroad and, while these players deserve tremendous credit for their contribution, it is my policy to bring the best available Scots to Tynecastle. That is why we moved quickly for the likes of Colin Cameron, Neil McCann and Jim Hamilton – players who had always impressed me and were at the right age to be given the opportunity to let their careers blossom at Tynecastle. As any manager will tell you, there is no magic formula . Once you have assembled the type of squad you want, it is then up to the players to deliver. We on the backroom team cannot play for them. They are brought here because we think they can do a job but if they do not deliver for one reason or another, there is no long-term future.

The Hearts way is about entertaining and that plays a

significant part in my thinking when I move for players. Joe Jordan had a fantastic spell at Hearts when he took them to the top of the league for a while, but there was something lacking – it was achieved in a style that was just not the Hearts. It was based on a more negative approach and they had curtailed their traditional style of attacking football. But that was his way, his own thinking and that is that. However, it is not my way. There are different ways to approach being a winner and I do things my way. People might not agree or like how we approach playing the game, but that does not matter to me. I stick to my guns; it's my job on the line and when you start listening to advice from so many different quarters then you are asking for trouble. I talk with my backroom staff, people like Billy and reserve-team coach Peter Houston.

We are all on the same wavelength when it comes to identifying the type of players we need and that's why we moved in quickly for McCann, a crowd-pleaser who burst onto the scene early in his career, making his mark at under-21 level and attracting a lot of attention in those early days with Dundee. Celtic looked set to move for him at one stage, but no one seemed prepared to fork out a transfer fee to take a chance with him and, with all that speculation about his future, the lad seemed to suffer a dip in form and lost his way for a while. We kept an eye on him all the way through, though I did think any hope of bringing him to Tynecastle had gone when he seemed to have set up a lucrative deal to play in Austria once his contract had run out at Dundee. Street rivals Dundee United appeared to have a big interest in taking him to Tannadice, but all through Jim Duffy tried everything to keep him at Dundee right up to the time he was set to move to the continent – he felt that McCann's heart was still very much for staying in Scotland. It was the scenario of a player moving abroad which would have left

Dundee with nothing in terms of a transfer fee. It was at the eleventh hour I stepped in and persuaded him and his agent, Blair Morgan, to come to Tynecastle for talks, and once he looked around the place he decided Hearts was the club for him. This was the bigger platform he had desired. Like any younger player, and particularly so in a winger, inconsistency was a big problem for him, but I knew that with the right handling and support he could emerge as a very great player with us. There were those who looked upon him as a replacement for Allan Johnston, but this was never the case. They are two totally different players – but both very good. Neil is an explosive player, while Allan had more intricate skills and fabulous close control. McCann is a very brave player, something in the mould of John Collins, slightly built but incredibly strong when on the ball.

Collins, of course, is a Borders lad who stayed only a stone's throw away from the home of Gala Fairydean. When he was a young player with Hibs I was the Gala manager and had his brother Norrie in my team – and the youngest of the family, Neil, was in the side I had in Lauder. John and I still keep in contact, and when I brought David Weir to Tynecastle, he told me soon afterwards that he found him the toughest defender in Scotland to play against. That was a telling tribute, in my book, for I think John Collins is one of the finest players this country has produced in a long time, a lad who is totally committed to his sport and thoroughly deserves all the success that has come his way. That friendship has helped me a few times; for instance, I did seek out his opinion on Stevie Fulton when I was interested in bringing him back to Scotland from Bolton Wanderers. John told me that in terms of sheer footballing ability Fulton had few peers, but Stevie appeared to be his own worst enemy for a long time in his career, failing to reach the level of potential to justify his natural ability. I knew all about Stevie's problem, but loads of people, including John, kept on telling me that if I could get through to him then I would have a top-class player on my hands. There was never any question of his ability, but the years were passing him by and it was simply not happening for him. It was difficult for him at Falkirk for, understandably, he felt it was not a big enough club for him – but he had to start somewhere to get his career back on track. He, no doubt, was of the opinion that he was doing me a favour by coming to Brockville, but when he was brought to Tynecastle he quickly started to realise we were doing him a real turn – the big stage that he had been seeking for a long time, to show that, after doing so well early in his career at Celtic – making his debut as a 17-year-old and winning honours at under-21 level – that he had made the grade at a higher level at the most critical time in his career. The challenge was to bring his skill to the full and make his mark on games by getting around the park, working his way into the danger areas and having shots at goal, instead of just shuffling around the middle of the park with the game going past him more often than not.

This laziness had people on his back all the time and Fulton could not handle that. Stevie could never be accused of cheating a manager, for the honest truth was that he was not physically fit enough to put in the work on the park that the modern-day game demands. A lot of people felt that he had a big chip on his shoulder but I never found that. Frankly, it did not go well for him in those early months at Hearts and I did detect he was starting to worry about it all. I think he realised he had to do it with Hearts or there would be no long-term future at Tynecastle. No doubt he had a little hint that I was not pleased with him when he asked me at training one day about his performances, as he was looking to sign a longer-term contract. The question was direct: 'Am I getting bombed out here?' I looked him in the eye and told him straight that the only person who was going to bomb Stevie Fulton out of Tynecastle was Stevie Fulton. I told him he would be given a new contract, but only on my terms, for I was not prepared to suffer what he had been doing in the first team for very much longer. He had to be told in no uncertain terms just how silly he was. Here we had a player with great talent who could find himself out of the game at the top level and he was still not even 30 years old. It was as simple as that: this was his last chance, for I doubted if any other leading club would show an interest and he faced playing out his career in the lower reaches, and that would have been a terrible tragedy.

There are no two players alike in football and that is where man management comes into its own, the judgement made by the backroom staff as to how to get the best out of an individual player, but still very much within the structure of the team. However, in the final analysis, it comes down to how the player reacts, he can either ignore the advice from those trying to help him or, hopefully, see the light and get on with changing his lifestyle. It was now all down to Stevie, and when he returned from the close-season break it was like a new man coming into Tynecastle. He had lost a lot of weight, looked absolutely great and, since that day, there has been no looking back. He trained like he has never trained before in preparation for the new season and I would imagine he was taken aback when I told him that what he had achieved so far had been first class, but the real challenge was being able to sustain it through the season. And, to my delight, he has done it, he thoroughly deserved a new contract for his contribution, for he is the player who can make things happen for a team. His fresh enthusiasm for the game, making the runs and starting to score goals from the middle of the park, brought him to the attention again of Craig Brown who had him in his under-21 squad. Craig brought him in for a couple of B international friendlies as part of the build-up to the World Cup finals in France, and Stevie did all right but just did not manage to force his way into the squad. However, I do feel if he has another good season at club level his chance in the full international team will come. Such was his importance to the Hearts team that I had no hesitation in appointing him captain for the Scottish Cup final when our skipper, Gary Locke, again lost out through injury. Stevie had deserved the honour for it had been hard earned over the season. Reward for effort is the basic ingredient for success in football. I'm sure very few people, including Stevie himself, would have thought he would have been the player to step forward to lift the Scottish Cup at Celtic Park. There was one magical moment which showed to me how much it all meant to him to be part of a winning Hearts side: he pulled Gary to his shoulder and they stepped forward together to lift the trophy. That was a spontaneous act by Stevie for there had been nothing prearranged by me in the event of coming out on top in the final.

The need for an influential Fulton was essential for the balance in the middle of the park, where I had initially moved him to bring in Colin Cameron – as I saw Colin as the catalyst to the way I wanted the team to play. It proved to be another piece of good business, a £225,000 fee to Raith Rovers with John Millar part of the transfer package. Colin looked set to join Aberdeen before I made the move just before the end of my first season at the club, and he has grown in stature with every passing season. He is one of the best in the business in getting forward quickly to link with the front players and show the bravery to get into goal-scoring positions. Colin carved a name for himself at Kirkcaldy and always came across to me as a winner, the type who will run all day for you and give his all to the team effort.

Jim Hamilton is another who I consider comes into that winners' category, a young lad who has brought himself to the fore with his goal-scoring feats at Dundee, playing alongside Neil McCann. It was essential to get in another proven goal-scorer, for the time was fast approaching when John Robertson was coming to the end of his career – with Hearts at any rate. It was not easy for Jim, or any player for that matter, in coming to Hearts as a striker, for he would be immediately compared with Robbo. It is only natural for such comparisons to be made but it is not fair to either player. Jim arrived as a raw lad with great potential who was still learning the game but with a totally different style to John. It was an exacting challenge for Jim to step up a league. He had been a regular with Dundee for a couple of years, but that did not mean to say he would step in straight away to the Hearts first team and become an established first pick. However, he has worked hard at his game and last season notched up 14 goals, which is a very commendable effort considering he was on the bench for quite a number of games. I look at Jim, as I do with a lot of the players we have at this club, as a player who still has a lot to give to the game. It is not easy for any player stepping up from a lower division and it does take some time to appreciate that there is no room for any player to 'switch off' in matches at this level. There is certainly much more to Jim's game now than when he first arrived. He is a more complete player and, when the need arises, he can drop back into the midfield position or even the back four, a position he played in his early days. He is tremendous in the air with a good footballing brain, part of a team that has been put together over the last three years for £850,000 and when they are all 'switched on' and performing as a unit they are a very tough outfit to overcome. The good thing for us is that all the players who have been brought in are at an age where they have still to reach their peak and, it is my sincere hope, that they can all progress together in the squad for a few years to come.

I feel it is essential for a club like Hearts to be very focused on ensuring that the cream of home-bred talent always comes to the fore. It has been a deliberate policy to recruit Scottish-based players with youth always to the fore. Having watched Hearts from afar for some time and aware that the club had won the BP Youth Cup and that they had always done very well in the reserve leagues, it mystified me as to why so few of the younger players were seen in the first team on a regular basis. It was reasonable to expect that some of the younger players would be starting to make their mark in the first team but it never seemed to happen. I found that difficult to understand. My theory on this is clear-cut: if young lads are doing well in the reserves but never seem to get a chance in the first they eventually hit a brick wall.

I know that from bitter experience as a young player myself. There has to be an 'out' after doing well in the reserves, otherwise your game will never improve. What all players need, particularly the younger ones, is to have a new challenge. If there is no light at the end of the tunnel, then there is no real point in having them playing in the reserve team in the first place.

In our situation – early on in my first season – bringing through the kids was the right thing to do. I was in a no-lose position but the response from the younger players at this club has been outstanding. The individuals have done well but there has been an equally important spin-off, other youngsters further down the line know that this is a club where the opportunity will come their way to make it into the first team. In fact, it goes even further down the line. Scouts know that their efforts will be rewarded: they will see young players getting their chance to come to Tynecastle because of the reputation that has been established over the last few years. The Hearts fans, by tradition, like to see young players come through the ranks and, to me, age is no barrier. If an 18-year-old is good enough, he will be in the team, just like the introduction of Gary Naysmith in the last year.

A club like Hearts must have an identity as being the club for youth, with the onus all the time on quality before quantity. The Scottish game and the standard of our emerging players has come in for a tremendous amount of criticism over the last few years and there is no doubt we have a problem. However, I must stress, I am firm in the belief that the talent is still out there, but not in such numbers as in previous eras. We are in a changing society with so many options open to the younger generation. We cannot do anything about that, but what we have to do is to ensure that we in football can come forward with a set-up that will encourage the kids to turn to football more and more. It is not going to be easy, but nothing in life is easy. The work has to be put in if we are to produce the next generation of good-quality footballers.

Of course, when a manager is making so many team changes in a comparatively short space of time, there have to be departures and a lot of good, hard-working, honest professionals have left this club over the last few years. No one likes telling a player that the end of the line has come but, in general, players know themselves that they are coming to the end of their time at the top level.

We've been through the tragedy of seeing Craig Levein having to give up the game through injury, and there is nothing worse than seeing a good servant like Craig being

Jim Jefferies with
school and youth
teams

ABOVE: playing for Hearts (front row, extreme right)
BELOW LEFT: a collector's item
BELOW RIGHT: playing for Berwick Rangers

HEARTS

MADE TO [...]

JIM JEFFERIES

PLAYER OF THE WEEK

No. 13 — JIM JEFFERIES
32-year-old Jim Jefferies, a regular at centre-half in our 1st XI this season, joined us in November 1981 from Hearts, where he had spent 12 happy seasons with the Tynecastle Club, and was club Captain for a considerable time. "Jeff" had previously played for East of Scotland side Gala Fairydean, where he had been farmed out by Hearts. He lives in Lauder, Berwickshire, and now works for Assurance Company Abbey Life, at their Edinburgh office, as does former Berwick player Paul McGlinchey. Jim and his wife Linda have been married for 10 years and they have one daughter, Louise, who is 2 years old. They have lived in Lauder for 10 years, although Jim originally comes from Wallyford, near Edinburgh. As a youngster he played with Gorgie Hearts, the Tynecastle nursery team. His favourite ground is Muirton Park, Perth. Jim won a Division One Championship medal with Hearts in 1979/80.
1st XI Record since signing: Games 51, Goals 0 (to Sat. 11/12/82).

HEARTS

15p

Heart of Midlothian Football Club Season 1978-79

CKAY BROS.
EDINBURGH

VEL · NATION WIDE CAR HIRE · MACKAY

V CELTIC
PREMIER LEAGUE
SATURDAY, OCTOBER 28, 1978. KICK-OFF 3.00 P.M.

Jim Jefferies, sprawling on the ground, features on the
cover of a Hearts match programme

The public duties of a Hearts player: in this case, it was opening a hairdressing salon

On their way to Leipzig: (left to right) Jim Cruikshank, Willie Gibson, Jim Jefferies and Cammy Fraser

Shouting encouragement from the dug-out
(© *Southern Reporter*)

Scottish
Brewers
Manager of
the Month

Proudly
holding the
Scottish First
Division
Trophy

The players and backroom staff line up to parade the
trophy around the streets of Falkirk

Jim Jefferies receiving recognition for all that he has
achieved with Falkirk

Training the Jim Jefferies way

forced into early retirement. His knee problems came right at the peak of his career. He was an outstanding defender who had deservedly won his place in the Scotland international team. He showed immense courage and determination to continue for as long as he did and there was no more sad a moment than when he announced his retirement. Fortunately, he is still involved in the game and has done a superb job as manager of Cowdenbeath, the club where he first started his senior career before he moved from there to Hearts for a little more than £40,000.

He was one of many who had a career with Hearts but never ended up winning a major trophy. Craig was held in high esteem by the supporters, and rightly so. All supporters have their favourites and there was none bigger than John Robertson. His popularity at Hearts is as big as at any other club, possibly on the scale of Ally McCoist at Rangers. To me John was the 'trophy' at Tynecastle, the trophy the club had never won in actual competition. He gave the supporters something to latch onto during the difficult times – they came to see him scoring goals. I know of supporters who came to Tynecastle to see only John in action.

I knew when I took this job that a series of tough decisions would have to be made about a lot of players and this is when you have to be strong and single-minded. Players had their own way of going about things, but I had to get the message across very quickly that they would all have to conform to my way of thinking, not the other way round. That is what management is all about. It was a tough decision, for example, to let a guy like Gary Mackay go after such great service to the club, he was always a Hearts fan who gave his all for the club as a player. I knew how much the club meant to him, how he loved the place, but at the end of the day it all comes down to a footballing decision, nothing more, nothing less. It is not easy to tell anyone that what they can give me at that particular point in their career is not good enough for me and my plans to take the club forward. What I had to do with John had to be done in phases . . . and he knew all along what was happening. What we are dealing with here is a player who will go down as one of the all-time Hearts greats. Just look at his goal-scoring record at Tynecastle. He will always be remembered by me as a very special player for Hearts.

John Robertson did well for me in my first two seasons and there was no doubt that he had earned a new one-year contract. It was made perfectly clear that he would be used sparingly during the season and, if he wanted regular first-team football, it was probably time to move. I also had to move forward, set plans in motion to have a team that could keep on progressing without John. No player, we have to appreciate, can go on forever, and plans have to be laid down to deal with that eventuality. Fans did not like it when John was often not in the team in the last season and I took a lot of abuse over his omission. No player likes to be left out of the team and they all handle it in different ways. Some bottle it all up inside them, while others bring out all the emotional hurt, as did John. That led to the well-publicised dispute we had right at the very start of last season when he was not in the starting line-up for the opening game against the reigning champions, Rangers, at Ibrox. We did not play well at all and, of course, there was a strong case for John to have played. That's the sort of thing you have to accept in management, but you have to be equally firm when problems do arise behind the scenes. That was the case with John, his head was down in training and I was not prepared to accept that sort of attitudes so he was asked to leave and train somewhere else. It was a simple thing, nothing exceptional, which happens from time to time at clubs everywhere and certainly no big deal or big issue. I felt action needed to be taken and I have done exactly the same with other players in the past. However, because it was John, it hit the headlines, but it was soon sorted out. I told him to stop getting upset, for this was a time when he should be enjoying his football. I have no problem with John, there never has been, but I am a very single-minded manager who wants to make this club successful.

In fact, the most helpful player to Jim Hamilton when he arrived here was John Robertson, good for him in training and in public and they worked well together. I think the fans started to appreciate just what we were trying to do with the team and John still had a contribution to make. He was a great option to have on the bench, but I knew he was coming to the end of his career at Tynecastle. I was going to have to be the manager to end a legend's career and, as we started our Cup run, I looked at John and knew how much he deserved to go out of this club as a winner.

He was great with the team in the Cup ties, full of encouragement all the time, for I think we all knew this was his last chance to come away a winner. As we all know, the dream came true at Celtic Park – even though he did not get on the pitch against Rangers. Let it be made perfectly clear that John was not in the 14-man squad for the final for any sentimental reasons. He was there to help us win the Cup. Indeed, John was the first to know that he would be involved in the final. I knew how much it would mean to him to be part of the squad and, when we were down at Stratford for our preparations, I could detect he was uptight and that made me decide to take the strain away from him by telling him he would be involved. The selection reason was simple; in the previous two games he had performed really well and in the game against Dunfermline I played him for a spell in a role which was slightly deeper than usual

– just off the front two – to see how it would go, for I was already thinking long-term about the final and what options would be open to me. When I told him he would be on the bench you could detect the release of tension, but that was a selection secret kept between the two of us until the team to face Rangers was eventually named.

Of course, it would have been the perfect ending for John to have come off the bench to play in the last few minutes, but, remember, we were under a lot of pressure near the end after that man Ally McCoist had brought Rangers back into the game. If we had been winning 2–0 with a couple of minutes remaining, then John would have been brought on. However, I know that he fully understood the situation and there was no problem on that score. I will always remember dashing onto the pitch to congratulate all the players for their glorious efforts and one of the first was John. 'Is this my last game?' was the question he asked me as we embraced in the middle of Celtic Park. But this was a time for celebration, to enjoy the win to the full, and I told him we would discuss that at a later date. Those talks took place at Tynecastle a week later and it was a difficult meeting. However, what was important is that we all agreed, John, his agent Bill McMurdo and myself, that this was the time for John to make his break for footballing reasons. He was going out as a winner. No player deserved that Scottish Cup medal more than John.

TRAGEDY AND TRIUMPH

For some years now, more often than not, the focus of attention on the pre-season build-up has centred around the massive spending by the Glasgow giants Rangers and Celtic. Last summer, the Old Firm splashed out somewhere in the region of £25 million for new players.

The player turnover at Ibrox and Parkhead has been quite remarkable – as has been our own since I took the helm at Tynecastle – but the rest of Scotland often looks on in awe at the financial investments these top clubs have made on players. Rangers alone forked out something like £15 million in team rebuilding as they set their sights on that record-breaking tenth league title in succession, as well as making an impact on the glamour scene of Europe, an arena we all want to play in and see European competition become an annual event in the sporting calendar.

Walter Smith reshaped his team almost every season and last summer he brought in the likes of Lorenzo Amoruso and Sergio Porrini to change his defence and, early in the league campaign, recalled former captain Richard Gough to help them out when they were ravaged by a succession of injuries.

The Swedish star Jonas Thern was also recruited, as was

Marco Negri, the Italian scoring sensation who had a quite incredible start – a double against us on the opening day of the season on his way to notching more than 30 goals before Christmas. Negri has had his critics but surely no one could possibly complain about his strike rate early in the season.

Celtic, on the other hand, had been clawing their way back from an uncertain period – by their own standards – and the recruitment of Wim Jansen, the first European coach to take the helm at Celtic Park, had sparked off a spending spree of more than £11 million, all part of the game plan to halt the Rangers dominance.

In came the likes of Danish international defender Marc Rieper, while Craig Burley returned to his native land from Chelsea and went on to be crowned the Football Writers' Player of the Year for his contribution to the success story of the season. Jansen also took Darren Jackson from Hibs, who overcame a frightening head injury and went on to play for Scotland in the World Cup finals in France; Regi Blinker came north from English football, while Scandinavians Harald Brattbakk and Henrik Larsson were brought in to provide the additional fire-power up front.

It is against this backdrop of money almost being no problem to the top Glasgow clubs that the rest of us have to endeavour to compete in the battle for honours. There are those who, in casting an envious eye at the constant influx of top players, see it as somewhat unfair – but I'll have none of that. I'm all in favour of clubs bringing in the best players that they can afford to the Scottish game, for there is no doubt that they expand Scottish football, and having no boundaries in the quest for talent can only help improve the quality of our football and give the fans the entertainment they are looking for on a Saturday afternoon.

We at Tynecastle have done not too badly in our recruitment policy over the last few years – my policy being to endeavour to bring the best Scottish players available to Tynecastle and look to augment that with moves into the continent, and beyond if necessary, in the non-stop efforts to continue to make progress. There are times when such transfer activity has to be put into perspective, and we at Hearts have spent around £850,000 on completely reshaping the playing personnel to try to take the club forward – and we have not done too badly so far.

With all the big-money men arriving at the two clubs at the western end of the M8, Hearts also signed three new players last summer and during the course of the season. The summer signing was Thomas Flogel, the Austrian internationalist who was a free agent under the Bosman ruling, and then we moved to bring in José Quitongo and Lee Makel – these two deals costing the club little more than £100,000 in transfer fees. That illustrates the difference when it comes to transfer activity but in no way makes me or anyone else feel inferior or jealous of what goes on elsewhere.

We get on with what we have got, set about moulding the squad into a team unit that plays aggressive, attacking football in a fashion that enables us to compete strongly with other clubs with ambitions to win silverware. The changes at Tynecastle have been quite immense and the season before last was a really testing time for us, for we brought in players such as Colin Dawson, David Weir, Stevie Fulton, Jim Hamilton and Neil McCann and it takes time for them to settle down and get into our way of working. This was all part of the long-term strategy to take the club forward. We had halted the decline in what had been a troublesome period for the club: two years of fighting tooth and nail against relegation and, in the season before I took over from Tommy McLean, Hearts had only survived after a good result on the last day of the season.

That was not what I wanted for Hearts. I had to change the whole strategy very quickly and get in the type of players I could have around me for a good few years, those with the potential to take the club forward in a big way and who would be looked upon as genuine competitors. I am not interested in being a one-season wonder, even after winning the Scottish Cup in May. We have to keep seeking improvement and we were very lucky in managing to get a player of great flair like McCann to Tynecastle. He was literally about to board a plane for Austria to seek to further his career before I stepped in. The then Dundee manager, Jim Duffy, knew that I had always been interested in the player and the circumstances were just right for me to move in. I quickly contacted his agent, Blair Morgan, a meeting was set up very quickly and he came to Tynecastle. Neil just needed one look at Tynecastle, hear what we were thinking about the future, and he quickly agreed to join us. He wanted to be with a big club and he saw Hearts as the right move for him.

But, for all the changes, that year we managed to finish fourth in the league and reached the final of the Coca-Cola Cup. Nothing was won but I was sure in my own mind that we were on the right road – but there was still a considerable road for all of us to travel. Missing out on Europe that second year was a huge disappointment, it was one of the few times that a team finishing fourth in the Premier League did not gain a place in the UEFA Cup.

While I had watched McCann for years and always wanted to have him in my team, the arrival of Thomas Flogel was something of a first for me: the first time I have ever signed a player without actually going to have a look at him. He was signed on a strong recommendation from one of my key contacts in Europe and Thomas, to be fair, has a great track record in the game and also has played for his country.

Dundee United were very keen to get him, but the late Brian Whittaker, a former Hearts player who had become a licensed FIFA agent, helped me to get the lad to Tynecastle for a few days' training. Sometimes in football you have to take a chance, a bit of a gamble on players, but I was quickly convinced Thomas could do a job for us.

I've managed to bring several players from foreign fields to Tynecastle, and probably Thomas has found it the hardest of all to settle into the way of football in Scotland. No two players are the same and it is often underestimated just how difficult it can be for players to quickly settle into a new playing environment in a foreign country. Thomas was a recognised international player in his own country and maybe, early on, he felt the game and the Hearts style should adapt to him rather than the other way round. Thomas is the first to admit that he did not make too good a start to life in Scottish football and he was terribly disappointed after his debut against Rangers on the opening day of the season and, frankly, I did not do him too many favours by playing him so early.

There's no doubt in my mind that here is a very gifted, richly talented player whose technical ability is as good as I have worked with anywhere, but I had to take him aside in training and tell him that he was looking like a fish out of water. He took it all very well and, while keeping him involved in the first team for training, I kept him out of the side to help with his readjustment to the way we play the game. Every credit to Thomas, he went away and sorted it all out and came back a very strong player, the turning point being his performance against Aberdeen at Pittodrie. Up until then Thomas must have been wondering if he had made the right move and I told him straight that this was his chance to get rid of all the frustration and show what he can do. I even broke with my usual tradition of not naming the team until the day of the game, to tell him on the Friday night that he was playing. I wanted him to be thinking about it, be mentally and physically prepared, and he came up trumps, scored two magnificent goals and displayed a lot of his superb skills. Of course, he ended up in the Cup-winning team, and I see him as being an important player for us in the future. He still has a year of his current contract to run but I am keen to persuade him to extend his stay at Tynecastle.

At the very same time, José arrived at the club. I know it was a signing that surprised many, for other clubs had looked at him, swithered about making Hamilton Accies an offer, only to back off. We had looked at our squad and felt José could give us something different. He is a player who is very difficult to pin down, with exciting skills, and the only doubt being whether or not he could play at a high level. We had watched him in high-profile games against Rangers and Motherwell and were impressed. We took up Hamilton's offer to have him with us on trial for a couple of weeks and, as has now been proved, he did have the ability to step up a level and turn a game with a touch of his magical skills. José is a player who gives us another option, another string to our bow, to give that added entertainment to our fans with the ability to either win matches or dig us out of a hole. He could not have wished for a better home debut than to come off the bench in an Edinburgh derby and score a match-securing second goal over our city rivals and, not surprisingly, he has since become something of a cult figure among our supporters. Players like José are good for the game and I will never duck the issue of taking a chance with a player who has such a great individual talent.

Nothing pleases me more than to see a player who has had it tough all through his life, grab the chance of playing at the top level. Everyone has taken to José but, mark my words, he is not as daft as some people think. He has his act, plays up to it, but, at the end of the day, has delivered for Hearts.

My other signing during the season also caused a bit of surprise when Lee Makel arrived on the scene. He was a player who was probably unknown to most football fans in Scotland, never mind Hearts supporters. However, he was well known to me and my backroom team for he had been a player we had first looked at more than three years earlier. In one of our many forays south of the border, this time it was a wet and windy night in Wigan and I was at Falkirk at the time, our initial target was Stevie Fulton.

It was a reserve game between Bolton Wanderers and Blackburn Rovers and the player who stole the show that night was Lee – the best player on the park. He had come to Blackburn for a lot of money from Newcastle United, for the then Rovers boss, Kenny Dalglish, quickly realised that here was an exciting talent. The lad won international honours at B level for England, but things did not work out as expected for him and he moved on to Huddersfield. He had a great time when Brian Horton, now manager of Brighton, was the boss and Lee was his midfield grafter. But a change of management, and the resultant change in the style of play, left Lee out in the cold. I made a general enquiry about his availability and it was only a matter of days later that we had him up in Edinburgh.

It was a big move for Lee but, like José, he was keen to accept the challenge. He has done really well for us in such a short space of time and while he did not make the Cup-final team, his chance will hopefully come in the seasons ahead. He's still in his mid-twenties, like many other players at Tynecastle, and we look at him – and the rest – as very much long-term investments and not as short-term measures to plug any gaps.

The way players have acclimatised to life at Hearts speaks volumes for the rest of the players at Tynecastle and their feelings for the club. It is all about building up a team spirit. Yes, there is a serious side to it, working hard in training and being of a mind to give your all, no matter the circumstances. At the same time you have to enjoy what you are doing and, at a club like Hearts, team spirit, a feeling of being happy in your work, is vitally important. We have players with an infectious enthusiasm for the game, one of the things we always look for when we are in the market to sign players.

There's nothing magical about our approach to signing players. Billy Brown and I both seem to have similar ideas on players. We don't always agree, but so far we have got it right more often than not. There is not much room for error at a club like Hearts, or most clubs in the Scottish game for that matter, where money is tight and we have to try to get it right virtually all the time.

My dad always taught me to back my own judgement and go with it. There are plenty of players out there who will give plenty of effort, run all day for you, but the ones who really make it are those with a football brain. This is not something you can manufacture, and when I look at a player I do focus on their thinking, the way they read and react to situations. We've had players like that at Tynecastle down through the years – great servants like John Colquhoun and John Robertson. It's this ability to do the right thing at the right time, to bring other players into the game, or hold the ball up, or take people on, that matters. In the later stages of careers I can also point out those with a footballing brain. When their legs will not take them into places they used to be able to reach with a sudden burst of pace, the brain takes over and they adapt and this keeps them playing at the top level for a lot longer. Thinking football is critical in the modern era, for the game is now so fast and those who can react the quickest will shine through.

These are the kind of players we have tried to bring to Tynecastle, creating the spirit and the commitment to work together as a team to take on the might of Rangers and Celtic. After all, as the old saying goes, it is only 11 against 11 when they cross the white line on match day. We have players at Tynecastle now who, on their day, can be as good as anyone else in Scottish football, no matter where they have come from. However, with more limited resources we are asking these same players, the McCanns, Fultons and Camerons, to turn it on week after week at the highest level. That, as anyone will tell you, is very difficult, but we have to strive for that level of consistency.

The start of last season was really no different to any other in terms of approach or preparation – or even the way we were going to play. I've never set definite targets; the only thing I look for is continued progress in what is one of the most difficult leagues to compete in.

I do not care what anyone else says, there is no doubt in my mind that there is a fear about playing in the Premier League. Some look at the Old Firm and all the money they have spent, or will spend in the course of a season, and set off with the fundamental thought of avoiding relegation. There is a school of thought at the start of every season that Rangers and Celtic will probably win all the honours and that has been the case in most seasons. All the clubs outside Glasgow have had a fright at some time or other; Hearts have been relegated twice from the Premier League; Dundee United have gone down; Aberdeen have been fighting for their lives in recent years; and now Hibs have dropped out of the top flight just as the new Scottish Premiership comes into being.

There was no doubt in my mind that this was a big season

for us. Most of the players had had a year to settle into the way of things and now we had to look to them to take their own game on and, in turn, set Hearts on the way to becoming serious challengers. The start could not have been more demanding, playing the champions at Ibrox on the night the championship flag was unfurled for the ninth time in succession and it was all being broadcast live across Britain on Sky Television. No one gave us much of a chance, but the bottom line was that we did not play well, it all being compounded by losing a dubious first goal at a time when Rangers were not causing us too many problems. Scoring a second soon afterwards virtually finished it in what was an indifferent start to the season.

We did not compete too well and the players were told in no uncertain terms what was expected. A team might have all the ability in the world but unless they put in the work they will never win anything. Players have to realise this. We then gave Aberdeen a 4–1 hammering in our first game at home, but just could not string two games together in the league – as was shown when we lost to Dunfermline at East End Park.

Then came the turning point for Hearts, and the entire season. Of course, it just had to be at Easter Road in our first Edinburgh derby against Hibs. They were on a high, off to a tremendous start, sitting on top of the league and their fans loving it. It was all there. Hibs had everything going for them and we were stumbling along and had just suffered that setback at Dunfermline.

Neil McCann scored the only goal of the game, but there could be no denying we were by far the better team and the winning margin could have been much more handsome. As the players came off the park, I knew within myself that we had something really special here at Tynecastle. The players had taken a bit of stick for their earlier performances, but their effort in that derby, a superb team effort, was really the launch pad for a remarkable season.

I felt that if we could put a run together we would soon be at the right end of the table and, when you start to get on a roll, anything can happen. Ironically, and it just shows how unpredictable this game is, we played some of our best football of the season and were knocked out of the Coca-Cola Cup by Dunfermline after extra-time at East End Park. No one hates losing more than me, but after the game I could not criticise a single player or the team performance. It was just not our night, but I told the players that if they played like that all season they would win a lot more than they would lose.

It was from then on that we showed our mettle, and the rest started to take note, when we defeated newly promoted St Johnstone at McDiarmid Park, picked up three points at home from Dundee United and then played some fantastic attacking football in successive away games at Kilmarnock and Motherwell – and scored seven goals in the process. That was the breakthrough, confidence started to ooze throughout the team and there was a feel-good factor in the dressing-room.

But what was equally important to me was that here was a Hearts team that was good to watch, playing the kind of attacking football that I would willingly pay money to see. That has always been my way since I started in management. I'm not one of those managers who believes in winning at all costs. I want to win by playing good football. That might be laughed at by some but I do not care. I do things my way and I feel it is the right way. Certainly, the reaction we have had from the Hearts fans has been tremendous.

My old mate Willie Gibson, a great striker for this club in his time, expressed his surprise at the way we play. But I have never been a believer in shutting up shop. Although I like an attacking-style of play, I'm not daft enough, at least I don't think I am, not to realise that we have to have things right at the back if we are to succeed and we have changed our defensive style considerably since I arrived here and that has not been easy in itself.

The younger players had been brought up on playing three men at the back, but I feel that that system has been found out, its lifespan has expired, and more and more teams are going back to playing a back four. That's always been my way and there is no doubt whatsoever that Paul Ritchie has come right to the fore this year because he is now comfortable in being part of a back four. He's thriving on the extra responsibility, there is no longer anyone behind him to clear up any errors, and this has made him a better player. He is now more aware of the game and if the ball now goes beyond him he knows it is his responsibility. All our training is about ball, ball and more ball, with the same emphasis on movement.

I'm not one of those managers who goes out of his way to study foreign coaches or watch videos for hours on end. I'm not perfect by any manner of means, I would never claim to be so, but I like to do things my way. Of course, you pick up things here and there but in football I believe you have to be your own man. Everyone has their own thoughts, beliefs and styles, and that is what we are eventually judged on. However, it is not down to just me, it is the way our thoughts are relayed to the players and how they react to what we are trying to do.

What we had achieved last season was not down to one person; it was down to a combined effort from us all and we kept on turning in the results, surprising more and more people on the way, until we came up against Rangers or Celtic in the league. We all know now that we never beat them in any of our eight league encounters – and that really surprised me. I've always had a decent record against the Old Firm, I won at Ibrox as manager of Falkirk, and the season before last we beat them twice in the league before losing to them in the 1996 Scottish Cup final.

This was the year when we really wanted to do well against them, particularly when we were right up there slogging it out with them for most of the season. I just cannot put my finger on it; maybe we just did not play well on the day or did not get the breaks where it mattered. I think the common denominator to all this was a realisation from within both Ibrox and Parkhead that Hearts were a genuine title threat. I think both Walter and Wim will concede that they played some of their best football of the season against us.

Even in the 5–2 defeat by Rangers in front of our fans at Tynecastle just before Christmas, Walter turned to me in the dugout as play raged from end to end and said he believed that anything could happen. To be honest, it could well have been 3–3 at the interval but the facts of the situation were that we were beaten. At the same time it was a recognition that Hearts were right up there. Rangers and Celtic knew that, but most of the pundits and experts doubted us and for weeks on end we lived with headlines all about the Hearts bubble about to burst. The constant criticism of the team was used in the dressing-room to spur on the players.

To their credit, the players showed they had the resilience to maintain the challenge and we battled right back after every Old Firm reverse. This was about the time of the season when my old pal Charlie Nicholas described me as a 'lucky manager'. To be fair, Charlie was not being detrimental towards me, but it was picked up by the media who put a totally different emphasis on the comments. I do not call it luck. If you work hard enough you make your own luck. In sport you need breaks along the line but they eventually even themselves out. I started my career at the bottom with Berwick Rangers and worked hard at the game. In golf they say you drive for show and putt for dough, but after ten years in management you cannot be lucky all the time. There's more to Jim Jefferies than luck. I've never doubted my ability in the game but, like everyone else, I will never stop learning or thinking of ways and means to improve my football team.

It was the team that kept us going in the title race right up until the last weeks, but it was a lot earlier when I knew within myself that measures had to be taken to give us that additional lift that we needed to stay right to the wire. We were right up there, but I knew months before that I had to try to get in at least one or two more players to give that added depth to the squad that I knew would be needed.

I made my move at what I considered to be the right time. We were flying, the team playing superbly well, and we were sitting at the top of the league. I went to the board and asked what could be done to bring in players. But at the end of the day it was simple finance – we either had the money to bring in new faces or we did not. I was asked by the directors what was needed and I told them what would really help would be the signing of two top-quality players.

They might not have walked into the first team straight away but they would have provided additional competition for places, which would have lifted those holding down first-team places and could well have spurred them on to produce even better performances. In this day and age it is all about depth of resources, for the demands on players are huge. I asked for the cash but they could not afford it. There was no fall-out and that was that. All my thoughts were about adding to the squad, not having to sell some of our best assets to raise the revenue to bring in others. That is not the way in which I want to take this club forward. Players coming in now have to be better than those already at the club, for in football you can never afford to stand still. What is for sure is that it gets tougher all the time.

We just had to get on with it but the signs were there – we were starting to struggle in games and scraped home. Yet the players kept up the fight, we went up to Tannadice when Dundee United were fighting for their lives, and we won 1-0, Jim Hamilton scoring the only goal of the game. The following Saturday in March came the big showdown with Celtic at Parkhead and we turned in another fine display to earn what looked like a superb away point at the time.

But then came the last half dozen games, and I do not think anyone could have envisaged that so many points would have been dropped by all three clubs in the title race. But the demands of the season were starting to take their toll and I knew there were players out there who, not through lack of effort, were unable to give of their best, mainly because they had been playing for weeks on end with niggling injuries.

Stevie Fulton was struggling, Neil Cameron was toiling with his pelvic problem, and the big game for us came right after our semi-final victory over Falkirk at Ibrox when Motherwell came to Tynecastle a few days later. The game was in doubt right up until the last minute and the terrible conditions made it a great leveller. I just hoped against hope that we would get a chance to nose in front. We did – Neil McCann scored the goal – and I prayed we would be able to hold out for victory. That was all that mattered, for it was that time of the season when all that mattered was winning. We made the mistake – and I stress 'we', for this is not the time to blame any individual – of going into our shell in the last 15 minutes and trying to defend. That is not our strong point, we are not that good at being totally negative; it is not our style. I just kept urging the players to keep the game flowing, get forward whenever we could. We stopped doing what we were good at and the ball was given away far too easily time and time again. We were retreating and this gave Motherwell, still battling for points to climb clear of relegation, fresh hope to come forward and eventually we were punished.

There were players out there who were not fully fit but we had to try to field our best team. But when our key players in the midfield area are not functioning, then the team suffers. When our field of Stefano Salvatori, Fulton and Cameron are on the top of their game then, as a unit, they are as good as any around in the Scottish game. They are absolutely vital to us for they run the game for the team both in terms of creativity and running power.

We came so close, but the demands of the season started to take their toll in a big way: we lost 2–1 at Easter Road; we were held at home by St Johnstone without a goal being scored; and then we suffered a three-goal defeat by Rangers in front of our own fans.

No one seemed to want to step out of the pack to lift the championship but, after a series of quite extraordinary results all round, Celtic eventually edged home to make it a joyous first season for Wim Jansen – not only by winning the biggest prize but denying arch rivals Rangers that record-breaking ten in a row.

It was an incredible league campaign, with an even more startling aftermath. The celebrations at Celtic's Parkhead had barely started when Wim Jansen left the club for good and returned to Holland.

But we had other things on our minds – the small matter of the Scottish Cup final against Rangers at Celtic Park on 16 May.

UP FOR THE CUP . . .
ALMOST

Reaching three cup finals in the three seasons since taking over is not a bad achievement by any standard, but just getting there, as any player or manager will tell you, is not good enough in itself when it involves a club of the status of Hearts, who had been in the doldrums for far too long.

Much has been said about these occasions being the big day out, a gala, a festival for the fans to savour and enjoy. For some it might be . . . but for me there is no worse feeling than losing a cup final and returning to that dressing-room when it is all over. It is a very empty experience, often very little is said as the celebrations go on in the other dressing-room at the end of the corridor. That compounds the hurt.

I've suffered such agonies as a Hearts player, I have been subjected to the same as a manager, and the pain does not get any easier. It hurts a lot to lose a cup final, nobody wants to know the runners-up. Cup finals are all about winning and it is only then that you can enjoy a big day out.

No one needed to tell me what agonies a club like Hearts have suffered down through the years, or how long it has been since a major trophy has been back at Tynecastle. I wanted to be the manager to win a trophy for Hearts, just like all my predecessors down through the years. Some had come agonisingly close, like Alex MacDonald in the 1980s; others had never even got near taking their team to a major final. Going to the final was, I have to confess, not one of my main priorities when I took the helm, for, given the state of the club and judging from their standing in the Premier League over the previous few years, the initial objective was to sort things out, make sure that top-ten security was achieved and then look to other things. I was well aware that the fans would give me time to get my own plans into action and that expectations would not be that high in my first season – but that never dented the long-term desire to be a winner. Any manager, no matter what job he takes, knows he has to reach certain levels to stay in a job in this highly precarious business. I knew, eventually, I had to deliver, but there was much to be done in terms of team reorganisation, both in terms of playing personnel and in the very style I wanted Hearts to play. That cannot be achieved overnight but I knew that, very quickly, radical progress had to be made.

In fact, my very first game in charge was a cup tie, a Coca-Cola Cup second-round tie against Alloa at Tynecastle and we did what was necessary – a three-goal home victory with strikes from Davie McPherson, Brian Hamilton and Scott Leitch. But from that very first game I knew things were not right and there was going to be a lot of pain and hurt. Our league form was so-so, a reasonable result here and there but there was absolutely no consistency to our play whatsoever and that was a worry. The next round of the Cup saw Dunfermline come to Tynecastle and we eventually managed to overcome a battling Dunfermline team, a club that has had a lot of criticism for their method of playing but most certainly not from me. Bert Paton, like the rest of us, had limited resources at East End Park, but he has brought the Fifers into the Premier League after the agonies of coming so close to promotion in successive years. Getting up there is one thing and, like I found at Falkirk, being able to stay up is a major achievement in such a cut-throat set-up. Bert and his players have managed to do that and what we call our 'other derby' is a really tough contest. That night in 1995 we won by a 2-1 margin, big Davie getting on the scoresheet again, along with Dave Hagen – his last goal for Hearts before being sold to Falkirk along with goalkeeper Craig Nelson as I set out to bring about change. However, our first visit away from home was the quarter-final tie against Dundee at Dens Park, the scene of one of the greatest-ever disappointments for Hearts in the modern era when the league championship was lost on Tayside on the last day of the season and Celtic celebrated with a dramatic, if not a shock, runaway victory over St Mirren at Love Street. It was to be another miserable night for us at Dens, a real roller-coaster of a cup tie before the game ended 4-4 after extra-time and we went out 5-4 on penalties.

That put paid to that and maybe it was just as well for I could not afford to let anything detract from our league predicament when we found ourselves rooted at the bottom of the league early in December. That was the crossroads for me and Hearts, the time for the shake-up had come and by the end of the year we had lost only two more games, to Celtic and Rangers – something familiar about that – but at least we were on the move and, by the turn of the year, despite a derby defeat by Hibs at Easter Road, I could see some light at the end of the tunnel.

I knew, however, that when we started to put together a few good results in the league that the fans were looking forward more and more to the Cup, but I never wavered from the need to make sure we did all right in the league, that would have been the trophy for me in the first year. But when the Premier League clubs went into the Cup draw in the third round we could not have been picked a tougher start, a home game against Partick Thistle, a team that were in the Premier League at the time and going along quite nicely but who we had beaten three times in the league before our Cup meeting at the end of January. It was a hard, closely fought contest all the way through but a goal from young Paul Ritchie took us into the next round. The victory was deserved and in the next round it was Kilmarnock at Rugby Park and the Ayrshire side were on the hunt for an Edinburgh cup double, having knocked out Hibs in the previous round. It was back-to-back fixtures against Killie in the Cup and the league and, to the credit of the players, they rolled up their sleeves and gained their just rewards with a fabulous double – the Cup tie being won 2–1 with Neil Berry popping up very late in the tie to give us victory. Confidence was growing all the time and going back down the following week to win the league match – John Robertson and Gary Mackay notching the goals in the 2–0 victory – was another tell-tale sign that things were starting to happen for us. Their performance showed me that there was a great determination about this team who were unwilling to accept defeat and showed they had the capabilities of fighting back when things were not running for them. I kept on saying to myself, the heart is getting back in Hearts. There was also, I am sure, a realisation from some of the other players, who were seeing all the changes that were being made and obviously becoming concerned about their own long-term future, that this might well be their last season to have any opportunity of cup glory as a Hearts player. We needed to be on the top of our form as the quarter-finals took us to St

Johnstone, a team under the leadership of Paul Sturrock, who were flying at the time in their own league and making a very strong bid to get out of the First Division and make a long-awaited return to the Premier League. It was played on a Thursday night at McDiarmid Park to suit the demands of Sky TV, but this is another change that the game has to learn to live with in the 1990s.

Again, big Davie McPherson came to the fore to deliver another vitally important goal for us as we edged out Saints 2–1 to set up a semi-final tie against Aberdeen, who were the clear favourites to topple us. Semi-finals can often be dreadful experiences and it has been a fatal round for Hearts down through the years when the club has stumbled just one game away from the final. It was a typically dour, tense confrontation with not a lot of good football played by either side. It was all about winning and, in what was a quite poor first 45 minutes, we managed to take the lead. While not playing that well we, nevertheless, looked reasonably comfortable as Aberdeen had to chase the game. It was not going too badly until Duncan Shearer came off the bench and scored the equaliser as the tie went into the later phase. But the lads kept their heads and, in the very last minute, John Robertson ghosted his way over to the left-hand side where he found space to deliver a superb ball across the face of the goal where Allan Johnston guided the ball past Michael Watt and into the far corner of the net. The place just seemed to erupt and the near-impossible had been achieved, a team that had been bottom of the league a few months earlier had made its way into the Cup final. It was a huge bonus and I knew that more than anyone. I was not being kidded that just because Hearts had reached a major cup final in my first season that it was all about to happen for us in a big way.

What we had done was to give the club and its supporters

some hope for the future and it was being done at a time of major transition with a lot of very young and inexperienced players coming into the first team. However, we were up against Rangers, a team at the very top of their form under the leadership of Walter Smith, but we had not done too badly against them in the league and, I have to be honest, I felt, against all the odds, we had a really good chance to beat them. The bottom line was that we did not play at all well, we held on until half-time when we were only a goal down, but Gilles Rousset made a mistake and that really was the end for us as we went on chasing the game. Every time we play a cup tie Gilles is always questioned about that error he made against Rangers in his first Scottish Cup final. However, never at any time has Gilles been blamed for that defeat by anyone at Tynecastle. He made a mistake and that was the end of it. The big man had done a wonderful job for us in his first season since his arrival from France and that was all that mattered to me.

Frankly, we were torn apart for the rest of the second half and the 5–1 scoreline was a right mauling. Gordon Durie and Brian Laudrup tore us apart on the break, Gordon scoring a hat-trick and Brian, so devastating when running at a stretched defence at pace, bagged a double. It was a terrible feeling after the game to have suffered such a heavy defeat and I really felt for our supporters as they made the long weary journey back to Edinburgh without the trophy. What I did tell the players before we left Hampden was that there is only one way to get the shock and upset of losing a cup final in such a manner out of the system, and that is to get back for another crack as soon as possible. Even with all the gloom and doom around me at Hampden, and during the bus journey back to Edinburgh, it really started to hit me that maybe, just maybe, we had the makings of a team to give them that trophy that they so desperately desired. Like me, they were tired of being labelled the nearly-team, the team with great supporters, but the team that just could not deliver on the day when it was winner take all. I had to take a cool, hard look at the first season and, despite the Hampden hammering, it had to be looked upon as a reasonably satisfactory start, given what faced me and my backroom team when we first took over. We had gone from the bottom to fourth and, in the process, won a place in the UEFA Cup and had gone all the way to the Cup final. Hampden was an experience that was hard to take but it was a learning process for a lot of us, and particularly the younger players. These sorts of big-occasion upsets can either make or break younger players and we had plenty of them in the Cup-final team. Having worked with them for almost a full season I knew they would handle it in the best way possible and be better for it. Sometimes you have to suffer quite badly in football to become a better player and there is no doubt in my mind my young lads have benefited. They did not want to suffer that again and have worked at their game all the way through and have improved with every passing season. There's nothing better than to see a younger player with great potential show the dedication and resolve to be a success in this business, and we have many at Tynecastle who are most certainly on the right track. Sometimes they slacken off a bit but, more often than not, a few well-chosen words sorts them out.

It is my philosophy in management that one change does not make or break a team but, without question, there are some judgements that are more important and prove to be more significant than others. When so many things were happening at the club, both on and off the field, I felt it was essential to show we were moving in the right direction, with a fresh approach and impetus, and one of the best ways to reflect that is in the choice of the team captain. Early on, my overall view was one of general despondency, almost a subconscious feeling that, although I would never accuse a player of deliberately not trying, things were not right. It is up to the manager to give a lead, go with his instinctive intuition, and I had to make a change in the captaincy. It was a new management team and the time was right for other changes – there were going to be no more hard-luck stories or any feeling that good fortune had deserted the club. I was having none of that; it was time to rid the club of the negative vibes. This was a new era, the club was going to be run my way on the playing side and, with so many young lads coming into the side, it was time to give someone else the captaincy and Gary Locke was the man for the job. He might have been a kid, but he was well respected and had such enormous enthusiasm to succeed in the game. Maybe the fact that he was a Hearts man, a Hearts supporter, had some bearing on the choice, but the overriding factor was that he was a good player and a player the fans could relate to as well. He showed very early on to me at Tynecastle during training that he had those inspirational qualities I consider to be so important. He took the responsibility in his stride, even seemed to grow in stature as a player and is someone who has never been afraid of telling others around him what he thinks. To be fair, the more experienced players reacted well to him, no doubt impressed by the fact that he was determined to be a winner and led from the front. He had an exceptional first season for me but then had that terrible setback on the biggest day of his life, the youngest-ever player to captain Hearts in a Scottish Cup final. He was really up for the final but, as we all know, he was caught in a tackle and had to be carried off on a stretcher with a serious knee injury which kept him out of the game for some time. His loss in that final was a huge blow but not an excuse in itself for losing so heavily to Rangers.

If ever a player suffered Cup heartbreak it has been Gary for he, sadly, missed out on the winning of the trophy two seasons later. He so desperately wanted to play at Celtic Park, and we gave him every opportunity to make it, but it was just not to be. It has been extremely tough for the lad but he has shown great courage. It would have been so easy to feel sorry for himself – and it happens to a lot of players – but Gary has the guts and determination to make sure that he comes back. It was not easy to tell him he was not going to Stratford to be part of our preparations for the final but he took it very well. However, when we returned to Tynecastle, I made sure that once the final decision had been taken that he had no chance of playing, he would still join the rest of the squad at Dunblane on the eve of the final. If ever a player deserved a medal then it is Gary, but I keep on telling him that his time will eventually come. Nevertheless, it is disappointing that some form of agreement cannot be reached between the SFA, the governing body who run the Scottish Cup, and the clubs, that extra medals should be struck for special cases. I agree wholeheartedly with the argument that there must never be any abuse of the system to in any way undermine the special nature of being a Cup winner. There's no need for any club to ask for five or six extra medals, but I do think a strong case can be made for an extra couple being provided in exceptional cases. For instance, there are players who may have made a major contribution in the earlier rounds of the Cup, but who were not able to participate in the latter stages due to injury.

There was one special incident that meant so much to me in the midst of our celebrations in winning the Cup: the gesture made by Stevie Fulton in calling Gary forward to join him in receiving the trophy. That told me so much about this squad of players that has been assembled at Hearts in a comparatively short space of time. The team spirit is second to none. That just did not happen nor was it manufactured. Spirit is all about picking the right people to have around about you, coming all the way from the backroom staff to the youngest player who has just been brought into the club.

It soon became clear to the players at Tynecastle that if they were not willing to conform to what we in management were looking for in terms of commitment to the club and their team-mates, then their careers would be very short-lived at Tynecastle. There are no places for such players in my team. I just laugh when I hear people suggest it is all about spirit and nothing else, and that spirit does not really count. That sort of attitude tells me that these same people, the experts who pontificate about the game, do not know very much about football and probably have never played in the senior game in any case. These people do the game a disservice. Football, from the lowest to the highest level, is all about spirit and is a major part of the game as far as I am concerned. I believe that everyone must be pulling in the right direction and helping each other out, particularly when a match is not going the way they would like. Players, for no obvious reason, sometimes go out on the park and have a bad day with nothing going right for them, no matter how hard they try. At such a time the last thing that is needed is for some smart-alec to get on the player's back and start dishing out stick. It's at times like these when the team spirit comes to the fore with the rest of the lads helping out in a positive way.

I really noticed a big difference in attitude after the first year I took over. Early on I could sense things were not right, and, after a sore 4-0 defeat by Celtic in front of our own fans, it was time to take the players away for a few days and start to put things to right before we played Hibs – the first derby for me as manager early in October 1995. It was a time for relaxation in the north-east of England, to train hard but with the opportunity to be together as a group. It just did not happen for I could see there were little groups here and others there, little cliques all round the hotel complex. That showed there was no togetherness and, in a bid to change it, I said to the players early in the week that the bus would be at their disposal to go into town to have a few beers on their own, so long as they were all back, no exceptions, at a certain time. Incredibly, there were no volunteers, the bus never moved from the carpark. It took me by surprise but there was devilment about them all.

I had to make it happen, dropping in a little word here and there to make sure the message got over that I could not believe they did not go out. Perhaps at the time they felt they were being true professionals in staying put and that they feared that I was putting them to the test. The rules are simple: everyone back at the right time and no one involved in any trouble. Anyone who steps out of line knows the score - fined two weeks' wages and, more often than not, left behind to make their own way home. This is all about man management and setting a common bond of understanding. Players respond to leadership and everyone has their own way of working, but I work from the basis of trust between us all with the management setting the lead. That was why Paul Hegarty was quickly brought in to join the set-up. Paul was to be the coach in charge of the reserves and youth teams. I suppose the move for Paul surprised a lot of people; he had no connection whatsoever with Hearts in any shape or form. However, this was someone who I felt was right for the club at the time to assume the responsibility for overseeing the development of the younger players. It was purely and simply a management decision in bringing to bear the knowledge of the game and observing the qualities of other people involved with other clubs. Paul had been a great player, won honours for his country, and had come through a hard school at Dundee United. He always struck me as a solid professional, a player who had looked after himself and someone who had always set a very good example – ideal, in my book, to bring out the best in young players and give them the encouragement and help to take their own playing careers forward in the way I would want it to happen. He had had a difficult time in management when he took over Forfar who, as we all know, are a part-time club. It did not work out for him there but, having spoken to him a few times when I was in charge at Falkirk, I was always impressed with him. Billy Brown and I are a close partnership but Paul was a completely different type to us and, for me, that is very important when it comes to putting a team together both on and off the field. He went on to prove to be another important link in the chain to take the club forward and when I made the first approach, Paul was desperate to come to Tynecastle and, having gone through the proper channels, the then Dundee United manager Billy Kirkwood told me he would not stand in Paul's way to move on to a fresh challenge. In fact, Paul could not get to the telephone quickly enough to tell me he wanted to come to Hearts. As is often said in football, he was over the moon.

As it turned out, Paul's stay with us was not for that long. Alex Miller, the former Hibs manager for a year, returned home from a stint as assistant manager to Gordon Strachan at Coventry City to take charge of Aberdeen after the departure of Roy Aitken. The first move in his plans to change things at Pittodrie was to move for Paul as his assistant. I did not want to lose him, but I would never stand in anyone's way when the opportunity comes along to take up a fresh challenge, particularly in the management and coaching side. The mere fact that Alex Miller, one of the longest-serving managers in the game and with a big

Falkirk days

Jim Jefferies with two of his new signings (© *Daily Record*)

ABOVE: the thrill of winning
BELOW: celebrating with the boys

Back at Hearts: (above) the rebuilding of the stadium, and (left) showing his true colours

A moment from the Rangers v. Hearts Scottish Cup final

The celebrations begin

Scenes of jubilation among the players and fans

Another game, another cup. Jim Jefferies' latest trophy

ABOVE: relaxing with friends and family
BELOW: whatever the weather . . .

involvement in the Scotland international set-up, moved for Paul was confirmation – if it was ever necessary – that Paul had a lot to offer the game in coaching. Paul and his family were our guests at the Scottish Cup final against Rangers and he joined in the celebrations back at Tynecastle on our return to the city. Indeed, I remember going up to Pittodrie not long after Paul had left us and one of the first people I met was his son Christopher in the corridor. He had loved coming to Tynecastle with his dad but there he was coming towards me to shake my hand, wearing that distinctive Aberdeen red top. I joked with him about it but he winked at me, lifted the jersey, and underneath there was a Hearts top. That impressed me, here was a lad who wanted his dad to do well at his new club but still remembered his time with us at Hearts. All these things are interrelated, giving an indication of the feeling and the spirit that we have tried to bring to Hearts – a club where all those involved, in no matter what capacity, can feel part of the set-up and can make a contribution. That togetherness is important to me, an essential ingredient, hopefully, taking the club forward on all fronts to achieve more success. Having the right management team in place is vital to the successful running of any club. Right now we operate with a team of three, Billy as my assistant, and Peter Houston in charge of the youths with Bert Logan, who has been the sprint coach to Hearts for 15 years, doing a great job for us behind the scenes in the preparation of the players to meet the physical demands of the Scottish game. Peter was a big favourite for a long time at Falkirk and when I moved from Brockville, given that Billy was already coming with me, it was impossible to take Peter with us as well, for I was anxious to give Walter Kidd his chance to work with me at Tynecastle.

However, Peter was always in my thoughts, we always kept in touch, and when Walter went to join Eamonn

Bannon at Brockville, my one and only move for a replacement was to turn to Peter. He was on a SFA coaching courses at the time, which forced me to leave a message with his wife, simply saying that I was looking for him. He probably knew what was coming and very quickly he was at Tynecastle and, now that Paul has gone, he has assumed total responsibility for the kids – and it is a job he does very well. My backroom team are given their head to get on with the job. I'm not a manager who interferes all the time but if I am not happy with certain aspects they are told in no uncertain terms. It is all about judgements; there are times to say nothing and there are occasions when I feel I have to step in and have my say. Hopefully, I am able to pick my moments and, in so doing, create the right impact at the right time. It is not a one-man show at Tynecastle, and never will be, so long as I am in charge. Possibly it is best summed up this way: Billy Brown is often asked from various quarters if he ever fancied being his own man and often he comes away with the statement that 'with Jim Jefferies you are your own man'. At times of change, and there have been plenty of them in recent times at Tynecastle, it is more important than ever to have the right backroom team in place.

For example, even before the Cup final against Rangers in our first year, we knew, no matter if we lifted the trophy or not, that there had to be further, rapid alterations to the playing staff. To get the club through the initial problems some initial signings were purely and simply short-term measures, fiddling around with the set-up to freshen things up here and there and always having to do it with little or no financial resources. Colin Cameron had been signed but could not play any part in our Cup run because he had been cup-tied with his previous club, Raith Rovers. But I knew he could be the catalyst to take us another step forward – and he cost me only £225,000 with John Millar going to Starks Park as part of the package. Cameron was the type of player to give us another dimension in the middle of the park, always busy and quite brilliant at his linking with the front men who were just settling into the club.

That victory by Rangers, with the loss of five goals, was never far from my thoughts all that summer and I was determined that it was never going to happen to me again. We might lose other finals but there was no way it would happen in such a fashion as that 1995 final at Hampden. I accept it had been a bonus to get to a final in our first season, but it was the result that hurt and hurt badly – losing five goals was devastating. Often you can go looking for excuses when you rerun the events of that afternoon but the bottom line was this – we had to take our medicine and get on with rebuilding Hearts and seek to get back to another cup final – and that target was achieved just a few months later.

The competition was to be the Coca-Cola Cup. However, before the end of August we had already made our exit from one cup competition, the European Cup-Winners Cup, against real quality opposition in Red Star Belgrade. The first-leg performance away from home in Belgrade was accomplished, a sound team effort in achieving a no-scoring draw to set us up for the return at Tynecastle a fortnight later. It was not our night, the return ended 1–1 – Davie McPherson scoring for us, but we went out of the competition on the away-goals rule and that put a real damper on our early season. That following Saturday we suffered a four-goal defeat at the hands of Aberdeen at Pittodrie. It was hardly a good preparation for our opening Coca-Cola Cup tie and another tough away game against St Johnstone. It was a testing game that night but we came away with a 3–1 victory after extra-time and we also needed an extra half-hour to overcome Celtic in the quarter-finals in front of a packed house at Tynecastle. It was always close but John Robertson popped up with a magical goal to take us into the semi-final. That meant we were to play Dundee at Easter Road. We had overcome our semi-final fear a few months earlier with victory over Aberdeen in the Scottish Cup. However, our form in the league was not that impressive until we picked off Celtic and we hit a five-game unbeaten run before the semi, beating Hibs 3–1 on the way at Easter Road, Cameron scoring twice and, of course, Robbo notched another derby goal to add to his record tally against the Hibs. This semi-final was against the same Dundee side who had knocked us out of the Coca-Cola Cup the previous season and there were a lot of people who were backing the First Division side to turn us over again.

However, there was no upset. The players turned in a highly competent performance, they scored early and took command of the game, playing some good football on the way to a convincing 3–1 victory – and the Dundee goal came from Jim Hamilton, who joined us at Hearts a few months later. Another barrier had been overcome; Hearts were through to another cup final and there, standing in our way again, was the all-conquering Rangers. It is worth reflecting on the team that went into that Coca-Cola Cup final and compare it to the one which lost those five goals to the Ibrox side just a few months earlier at Hampden Park the previous May.

For Hampden we started with: Rousset, Locke, Ritchie, McManus, McPherson, Bruno, Johnston, Mackay, Colquhoun, Fulton, Pointon.

The team for the Coca-Cola Cup final was: Rousset, McPherson, Pointon, Mackay, Ritchie, Bruno, Paille, Fulton, Robertson, Cameron, McCann.

This is a true indicator to the massive turn around in playing personnel in a very short period of time. No one would ever underplay the achievement in reaching a Cup final, but all along I was acutely aware of was the need to bring in new players to improve playing standards, this would enable the team to make further progress.

Here was another final challenge for us, at Celtic Park this time – and remember, the game was in doubt right up until the last minute because of the snow. It was a dreadful day to watch football but Celtic Park generated a great atmosphere for the final, and what a remarkable game it was against Rangers. Yet, it was another nightmare start for us. All the preparations, the plan to adopt a slightly different approach after the hammering in May, counted for nothing, in fact, it virtually went up in smoke when we lost a goal early on. We played four at the back with five across the middle in a bid to make it hard for Rangers to break us down, but then it all went badly wrong and I am sure many thousands of Hearts supporters looked upon it as: here we go, another drubbing for Hearts at the hands of Rangers in a cup final. Two goals down after the first 16 minutes which left us chasing the game and it was a huge mountain to climb to get back into the contest . . . but the players responded quite brilliantly. We battled back, Stevie Fulton got us going with a fine goal just before half-time and we firmly believed that if we could get back on level terms we would go on, against all the odds, to win the Cup. However, the one thing you cannot legislate for is the brilliance of Paul Gascoigne and, on the day, he won the Cup for Rangers.

We got back to 2–2 and the Cup was for the taking but then Gazza took over, a touch of magic, coupled with what we considered to be a very harsh decision by referee Hugh Dallas going against us, changed the entire final. The refereeing decision I'm referring to was an incident right in front of us in the dugout in front of the main stand. John Robertson was first to the ball and could have let it run out, but opted to nick it past Jocky Bjorklund as he moved in to tackle him. In our view it had to be a foul when the Swedish defender made contact but the referee thought otherwise – and he is the man who makes the decisions. He waved play to go on. We were to a man in claiming a foul. For a split-second concentration was lost, and the rest is history. Gascoigne picked up the ball, took on our defence and scored a quite magnificent goal. It was a superb piece of finishing from a really top-class international player and he struck again to give his team a 4–2 lead and, while we did pull a goal back, we did not have the time to get back into the final. It was another cup-final setback for the club and its supporters who again left Glasgow empty-handed. But to me the team showed not only character to come back from such a double blow from Gazza, but displayed all-round improvement, the mark of the progress of the team was there for all to see.

One of the most significant comments to be made after that final came from none other than Rangers manager Walter Smith. He looked upon Hearts as a team with the spirit to go on to do well and he predicted that, within a year, Hearts would fulfil their promise. Those were words I took on board, for Walter is one of the men I have the utmost respect for in Scottish football. We go back a very long way, even playing in the same era, and I often recall a moment many years ago when we captained our respective teams, Hearts and Dundee United, in a reserve cup final at Tynecastle. We managed to beat United that day to win the trophy and one of the first men to come over to congratulate us was Walter. He even went out of his way to seek us out after the game in a little players' room, where the ticket-office is now located in the administration block. He stayed in the game and eventually joined Graeme Souness as his assistant at Ibrox at a time when I drifted out of the senior game for a few years and pottered away for a while in the Borders. But we never lost touch with each other and, in fact, he was one of the first people I spoke to when the management offer came from Hearts.

Walter has never changed from the day I first met him. He graduated to become manager of Rangers but he always had time to speak to me and other managers, no matter the circumstances or the outcome of any game. Walter is always the same in victory or defeat, a very nice guy, always full of encouragement, and he will never walk past you. I have only one view about Walter Smith as a manager – he is the very tops. Football, as we know, is all about opinions and every section, be it managers, coaches, players or supporters, do not agree about things and that is the way it should be. That is what makes our sport so special and we must all work to foster our game. There are those who try to knock Walter and Rangers, many moaning that it is not a level playing field because Rangers have the money to buy all the best players. But I cannot understand people who try to blame Walter for that. It is an absolute nonsense. Walter had been good enough to get the job as manager of Rangers in the first place and he has spent the money available to him very well. Just look at his track record and the players he has brought to Scotland, players of the highest quality like Brian Laudrup. He brought Paul Gascoigne to Scotland after most people were writing him off after what had been a difficult time for him in Italy. He came to Rangers and did a good job for them. No one can take anything away from Walter. He was given the money to bring in players that would win titles and cups. When he took over from Graeme it was a hard task but he has done a truly magnificent job as his record illustrates: seven league championships on the way to the record-equalling nine in a row and six cup-final triumphs – three League Cups and three Scottish Cups. It does not matter if a player costs £5 million or £50,000, the manager still has to manage them and integrate the player into a team plan. Money does not buy you success, as has been proved at many other clubs down through the years. What it does do is give you a better chance to reap success – provided that talent is able to be gelled into a good team unit. You do not put 11 players out on the park in this day and age and just tell them to play. It does not happen that way.

It was particularly pleasing for me to follow in Walter's footsteps this year as Manager of the Year and it was somewhat ironic that our Cup-final triumph at Celtic Park, Walter's last game in charge of Rangers, would deny him a trophy for the first time in 12 years at Ibrox. It was a disappointing Cup-final day for him, but Walter was first to come over to the Hearts dugout to congratulate me and the rest of the staff. I knew that he would not be out of the game for that long once the season was over. Walter might have been retiring as manager of Rangers but there was no way he was retiring from football. I said that on the night I picked up the Manager of the Year award in Glasgow and that is exactly what has happened. Everton now have Walter and Archie Knox and the Liverpool club are very lucky to have this management team. I am glad he has gone to Everton, he is now on level terms with many of the bigger name clubs in the English Premiership when it comes to spending money on players. Some might look upon this as the true test of Walter's ability as a manager but there is no doubt in my mind at all that he will be a success in English football.

He's got a rebuilding job to do – just as I still have, one that has been going on for three years at Tynecastle. That middle season at Hearts, even in reaching the Coca-Cola Cup final, was always going to be a difficult year for us. I know some of the fans looked upon two cup finals in six months as huge steps towards making the trophy-winning breakthrough, but I never looked at it in that vein at any time. It was still a building process, the foundations, in my view, at that time were hardly dry and there was much to be done in so many areas. No way were we coming close to being the finished article after winning the Scottish Cup. What the cup runs did was provide me with essential finance to be able to do deals here and there on the transfer front so that I could bring in players to add another piece to the team-building jigsaw. The team was funding itself, but that middle season was very much up and down – it showed that we were too inconsistent to be a real threat to anyone in the upper half of the league. That was well illustrated when we went out of the Scottish Cup early. We opened up with a five-goal victory over Cowdenbeath at Tynecastle, but then went out in the next round to Dundee United in a replay at Tannadice.

We had never lost sight of the fact that we were still tinkering with the team, yet we still managed to finish fourth in the Premier League. Alas, that finish was not good enough to give us a place in Europe the following season and that was a huge disappointment to me. We had been looking for Dundee United and Celtic to make it to the Scottish Cup final, but it was a year of upsets with Dundee United falling to Kilmarnock after a replay at Easter Road. If that was a surprise it was nothing compared to the happenings at Ibrox. Celtic against First Division Falkirk was looked upon as a non-contest by most. When Falkirk drew on Saturday it was thought their chance had gone, as you don't get a second chance against the Old Firm! What did Falkirk do? – they returned to Ibrox and defeated Celtic and that was probably the result which cost Tommy Burns his job as manager at Parkhead. But out of the Cup-final upsets, Hearts were the losers – all hopes of playing in

Europe had gone. It was a timely reminder to me, and everyone else at Hearts, that in football you cannot rely on anyone to do the job for you: it has to be done by yourself. We had enjoyed our one-match taster against Red Star Belgrade in the Cup-Winners Cup the previous year and we wanted more. A club like Hearts needs to be involved in the European scene on a regular basis. It has been a bonus in the past but, eventually, we must strive towards it being a regular occurrence, a feature of the footballing calendar at Tynecastle. Like everything else, it has to be earned on the field. No one gives you anything in football and there is no tougher set-up than a ten-club league where competition is intense and getting more so with every passing season. It does sound a bit boring, but I never stop preaching to my players that consistency of performance is the only way to win things in football. There is no doubt in my mind that we have players at Hearts who have the ability to hold their own with the best in Scotland – but there is no point in me just saying that. It all comes down to actions on the park, marrying that ability with the determination and the commitment to success. Football is about hunger and desire.

We still operate in a limited market when it comes to signing players but there is little that can be done about that – in the hard financial reality that has to be accepted. The more we can keep the squad that we have built so far together, and it is a very young squad, the better they should eventually become, provided the professional application is to the fore all the time. There are players I would love to bring to Tynecastle and it does get a bit frustrating at times that we cannot get them. But, as I have said, I knew the score when I took the job in the first place and I just have to get on with it. This is a big club that I want to make even bigger and for it to be up there year after year competing hard for all the top honours. I think I have shown that I do have a reasonable track record in building squads with very limited resources at the time. Of course, I would love the day when I could go out and bring recognised big-name players to Hearts. We would all want that – everyone connected with this club from the boardroom down. Circumstances are changing at the club, things are getting better all the time. I would like to think that the day will come when I will be handed a lump sum of money, for me to spend just as I wished to bring in the players I thought could take the club up another step of the progress ladder. It would be nice to have that big-money option, cash to be used to buy one player, two players or even ten players if that is what I wanted to do. Certainly, I do not think there could be any complaints from the board of directors over the level of success we have enjoyed so far, especially considering what has been spent on the team – all of which has been achieved for around the £850,000 mark over three years. That is good business by any stretch of the imagination. But it is not all about buying and selling, one of the big plus factors at Tynecastle is the quality of the young players who have come through – and they all want to play and do well for Hearts. Over the last few months we have been able to agree terms with Gary Locke, Paul Ritchie, Gary Naysmith, Stevie Fulton and Colin Cameron to extend their contracts into the millennium and that has to be really good news for the future of the club. They have shown the level of commitment that is needed in football and the current Hearts squad, it should not be forgotten, is one of the youngest in the Premier League.

The football scene has changed quite dramatically over the last few years in so many different ways and none more so than when it comes to the buying and selling of players. It all stems, of course, from the Bosman ruling. Before, we had the strange scenario of players going out of contract and moving abroad to play – John Collins leaving Celtic for Monaco is a perfect example – without any transfer fee being involved while such a player could not enjoy that option in Britain. That has now changed and we, at Hearts, were the first to make use of the new rule to bring Steven Pressley to Tynecastle from Dundee United. That move has worked in our favour but there will no doubt come the time when it will go the other way and we will lose a very important player to another club, in Scotland or England, for nothing. It is yet another difficulty for clubs. Steven no doubt looks at Hearts as a team on the move and wants to be part of a squad that can mount a big challenge to the likes of Rangers and Celtic. The arrival of Pressley gives us more options, for the modern-day game is not just about 11 against 11 – it is more and more focused on the squad system. We are getting nearer and nearer to having that depth of resources and there are no borders when it comes to the recruitment of players. We've a lot of good home-bred kids but we keep on looking to Europe for young players as well. In the summer we brought in two youngsters from Austria, Christian Schandl and Markus Holemar, on short-term contracts. They both wanted to come to Scotland to play for Hearts and, if they fit the bill, they will be offered longer-term contracts to be part of the on-going Hearts revival.

HOME WITH THE CUP

The Scottish Cup remains the one tournament which gives every club the opportunity to have their big day in the soccer sunshine, and long may that remain the case in this era of quite remarkable change as far as the senior game goes.

Years of campaigns to change the senior set-up – particularly the top level of the sport – suddenly came to fruition earlier this year with the establishment of the Scottish Premier League, a new organisation which has won the right to run their own affairs and have command of their own destinies. It is an exciting new era with massive sums of money coming into the sport with Sky Television clinching a massive £45-million deal for live coverage of 30 league games every season for the next few years. The tradition of playing the big matches on a Saturday afternoon has gone and now we have the set-up of playing live television games early on a Sunday evening with a 6.05 p.m. kick-off. I have no complaints about that, we have to move with the times and have the set-up whereby the game at large can benefit from much-needed financial investment. We all want to see the standard of Scottish football improve by leaps and bounds as we approach the millennium and we

141

all have a role to play at every level in the sport. I'm at the sharp end, in having to endeavour to continue to bring success to Hearts, and that is no easy task when you are facing the might and the spending power of Rangers and Celtic who, as we know only too well, have greater resources at their disposal than the rest of us put together.

However, we must never lose sight of the fact that football is the game of the people and that is why the Scottish Cup must always remain as an integral part of the sporting calendar. It is the only tournament which opens the door to all clubs to participate and gives them the opportunity to pull off one of those famous giant-killing acts at the expense of one of the senior teams.

We, in the Premier League, only come into the tournament in the latter stages, which is usually sometime soon after the turn of the year – but for others it has been a long and arduous campaign which starts very early on and sees a variety of competitions. The North and South of Scotland Qualifying Cups are the avenues for the clubs in the lower reaches to make their way into the tournament proper; I know only too well how much it means to those little clubs all over the country when the tournament gets under way – I've been there, I've seen it and I have done it. Not many managers in the Premier League can say that, that is probably why the Scottish Cup will have a special place for me every single season. I remember going into the tournament as manager of Gala Fairydean, and I have been aware of the massive interest it creates in communities outwith the mainstream of football for a couple of weeks a year. It is important that this continues in order to give these smaller clubs the target they all need, that special challenge, to pit their wits against opposition from the higher leagues.

It might be easy for some to sit on high and pour scorn on the need for such a competition, but there is no bigger talking point in the game than when there is a major upset. It's more than 30 years since the greatest shock of all time: when the great Glasgow Rangers went down to Shielfield Park and were knocked out of the Scottish Cup by Jock Wallace's Berwick Rangers. That feat is still talked about today, and that same excitement will always surface any time a so-called minnow is paired against a big gun in succeeding competitions. To me, that is what the game is all about, it is the uniqueness of the Cup.

Before we entered the fray towards the end of January, the first two rounds proper had been completed and there were the usual shocks along the way. This time there were to be no heroic acts from Whitehill Welfare who, just a couple of years earlier, had been paired with Celtic and met at Easter Road on a never-to-be-forgotten day by the Midlothian village. This time, however, they made an early exit at the hands of Inverness Caledonian Thistle in the capital city of the Highlands. However, the spotlight was grabbed by Edinburgh City, the famous capital club who had fought their way back from the brink of extinction and made it into the second round and a tie against East Stirlingshire. The match at Firs Park ended in a no-scoring draw, but Gordon Rae, the former Hibs star, led his part-timers to a fabulous replay win after a dramatic penalty shoot-out at the Commonwealth Games stadium in Edinburgh, which set them up for a dream tie against Dunfermline. To get there was a fantastic achievement and I know the lads had a super day out even though they lost 7–2 to Dunfermline Athletic.

The only thing that matters in the early rounds of the Cup, no matter the opposition, be it Rangers or Berwick Rangers, is having a home draw, and our entry into the competition in the third round saw us paired with Clydebank at home. There were no thoughts of the final in our minds, it was all about the job in hand, getting over the hurdle to make sure we were not going to be the fall-guys. We had to make changes for the game, some forced and others with a view to giving different players the opportunity to play from the start. It was all about making full use of the squad at a time when we had recovered well following the 5–2 defeat by Rangers in the league in front of our fans, an incredible game which I still believe to this day could have gone either way. Yet, credit to the lads, they took the knock on the chin and bounced back with a very competent away win over Dunfermline at East End Park, only to surrender a two-goal lead in their New Year derby with Hibs and having to settle for a point. However, we remained unbeaten in our successive away matches against St Johnstone and Kilmarnock before the Cup tie. We were without goalkeeper Gilles Rousset, that opened the way for Roddy McKenzie to play for the first time that season and we left Colin Cameron, John Robertson and José Quitongo on the bench. We were never really under any major threat all through and goals from David Weir and Thomas Flogel edged us comfortably into the fourth round.

At the same time Rangers had a fight on their hands overcoming Hamilton Accies at Fir Park, Motherwell; while Cup-holders Kilmarnock eased their way past Stranraer; poor old Hibs, having a torrid time in the league, were tumbled out of the tournament at home by Raith Rovers – it was another shattering blow for them; and Motherwell needed a replay before beating off the challenge from little Dumbarton. As ever, the Cup was coming to life and the big shocks were yet to come as the Cup-holders found to their cost. It was the upset of the tournament when Killie met Ayr United in a derby mud bath at Somerset Park and Bobby Williamson's side were bundled out by their rivals from a lower division. The pain of defeat was etched all over Bobby's face as he talked about losing their hold on the trophy. At the same time Hearts were in action back at Tynecastle against Albion Rovers from the Third Division and they had been given the utmost respect from us. They had been watched by our scouts for a couple of weeks and Billy Brown took the opportunity to have a look at them in a midweek game against Cowdenbeath, who are now managed by Craig Levein and who has done a great job in his few months at Central Park in reviving the club – with a little help from one or two of our younger players who were put out on loan to the Fife club to help them gain much-needed competitive experience.

Gilles was back in goal for the Albion Rovers tie but, due to injuries, we were without the important trio of Gary Locke, Dave McPherson and Stefano Salvatori for the home tie and, in fact, our skipper Gary was to play only four more games in the league. However, the lads did what was required of them in the tie, with José Quitongo scoring his first double for the club and Colin Cameron also on the scoresheet, as we cruised to a three-goal victory without conceding anything, which was just as important to me. If we can keep it tight at the back, no matter the opposition, then we have the players with the guile and craft to score goals at the other end. A last-eight place had been secured and, at that stage, we were heavily involved in the chase for the league championship alongside Rangers and Celtic. The Old Firm did not have it easy in that fourth round, Rangers having to fight all the way to secure a 2–2 draw with Motherwell at Fir Park before sweeping to a comprehensive three-goal victory in the midweek replay, Jorg Albertz scoring two cracking goals with the other counter coming from Gordon Durie. Celtic, meanwhile, had a Sunday tie against Dunfermline at East End Park but found the resolve to overcome this difficult hurdle 2–1; Stephane Mahe and Harald Brattbakk netting the goals that mattered. Of course, the shock of the initial ties was the courageous display by Inverness Caley Thistle against Dundee United. The newcomers to the Scottish senior game earned a superb draw at Tannadice, one of the hardest grounds to get a positive result at – as I know only too well – to take the top-ten side back north to their new stadium on the outskirts of the city. They certainly gave their all, took the game into extra time, but lost out on the narrow 3–2 margin.

It was fast emerging that Ayr United – one of the teams causing the upset – were paired with us in the next round. Ayr United were our opposition at Tynecastle with a place in the semi-finals beckoning the winners. The Somerset Park side were full of confidence coming to Edinburgh on the back of knocking out the Cup-holders and we knew we had to be up for this one, right on top of our game if we were to reach another semi-final. We had every reason to feel in the mood to see off the Killie giant-killers for we had come off a series of very good results in our ever-strengthening league campaign. We had gone to Motherwell and scored four goals; beaten Aberdeen 3–1 in front of our own fans; and then had a tremendous performance against Rangers at Ibrox, but a 2–2 draw was scant reward for the way we played, Jim Hamilton and Neil McCann being our marksmen while Jorg Albertz was the Rangers saviour with a double. Nevertheless, we did not take long to jump into the lead in the Cup tie with a superb strike from Paul Ritchie, a superb piece of opportunism, to lash the ball into the roof of the net. Ayr were reduced to ten men and that certainly helped our cause, but there was a minor scare when former Hearts man Ian Ferguson scored a goal for the never-say-die Ayrshire side. However, we were just too powerful for them and we ran out 4–1 winners to book our place in the last four – but we had to wait a while to find out the other semi-final participants. Falkirk, beaten finalists the previous year, were very much up for the Cup and they stunned the much-fancied St Johnstone with a great win over the Premier League side at Brockville. I watched a video of the tie soon afterwards and no one could deny my old club another Cup scalp. Alex Totten had his side fired up for this one and they completely overran the Perth side with a remarkable three-goal victory and the dream lived on for the First Division side to make the Scottish Cup final for the second season in succession.

It was another bumpy ride for Rangers at Dundee, at a time when Dundee were in a commanding position in the First Division and well on course to gain promotion to the new Scottish Premier League for next season. When Dundee came to Ibrox they produced a highly competent team display to hold Walter Smith's side to a no-scoring draw. That set up a bumper few days in Tannadice Street. Before the replay Celtic had to face Dundee United in a live TV quarter-final and it was a five-goal thriller with Wim Jansen's side edging home by a 3–2 margin. Now it was the turn of Rangers to take up the challenge of keeping their trophy-winning dreams alive at a packed Dens Park. It was a fantastic cup tie, full of thrills and spills all the way, but cometh the hour cometh the man and it just had to be Ally McCoist to score the victory double to take Rangers into the last four. What a fabulous servant Ally has been to Rangers, an incredible goal-scorer but a player who, usually through injury, has been used sparingly throughout the season. But if Rangers needed someone to dig them out of a potential trouble spot, then Ally is the man – and he did it in style at Dens that night. Ally has been an Ibrox hero down through the years and he thoroughly deserves all the adulation. His goal-scoring record speaks for itself, as we at Hearts have often found to our cost, and he was yet to cause considerable heartache before the campaign was over.

The scene was set for the semis – and we got the draw we wanted: Falkirk at Ibrox. The other semi-final was a battle of the Old Firm, Celtic against Rangers at Celtic Park.

I'm sure Alex Totten and his Falkirk players were equally happy to have been paired against us and, of course, it brought me and Billy back into the firing line after our long connection with the Brockville club and our subsequent departure for Tynecastle. That all added a bit more spice to the occasion and I knew that matter would be brought up time and again in our run-up to the tie. It was a situation I just had to take on board but never at any time did I let that undermine the most important matter of all – beating our opponents to make our way into yet another Cup final. Frankly, my thoughts were concerned with what Falkirk had achieved on the park 12 months earlier.

They had gone to the same semi-final venue, Ibrox, as the underdogs, rank outsiders, for the tie against Celtic. What they achieved then was quite magnificent in anyone's book – not only had they held Celtic to a draw in the first game, but then went on to win the replay to make the final against Kilmarnock. I knew they would jump at the opportunity to grab that 'underdog' tag and use it to their advantage. It was an obvious ploy to put us under added pressure. There's no doubt they fancied their chances. After all, if they could see off Celtic, with all the high-quality players they had at their disposal, meeting us – who they thought were a weaker opposition – would be seen as a great opportunity to complete a great Cup victory double. Make no mistake about it, the pressure was on us from all sorts of areas. Here we were in another semi-final, the expectation had been growing all the time, yet so often this stage in cup competitions has been our graveyard on more occasions than I care to remember. Again our bottle to cope with the demands of the contest was brought into question, just as it

had been for months on end during our league championship challenge when we were right up there with Rangers
and Celtic and always looked at as a third force, the no-
hopers in the eyes of most.

It was very important that we prepared properly, to be
completely focused on the job in hand and, as usual, we took
our players away for a few days. Unfortunately, all through
our build-up there was the nagging concern over the fitness
of Stevie Fulton who had been struggling for weeks with an
injury but who bravely kept on playing and, in fact, won his
way into the Scotland B team for the friendly against Wales
at Broadwood Stadium in Cumbernauld, the home of Clyde.
It was a richly deserved reward for an outstanding season
but the stress and strain of a very hard and demanding
campaign was starting to take its toll. I had been aware of
the problem, but Steve was such an important player for us,
and so, all week we nursed him along in the hope that he
would make it. We delayed and delayed before giving him
the critical fitness test on the Saturday morning just before
we left for Ibrox. It was a major blow to lose him and the
decision for me was to come up with a replacement to keep
the balance of the side right. Eventually, it boiled down to
two players, Thomas Flogel or Lee Makel – the young player
we had brought to Scotland just a few weeks earlier from
Huddersfield Town, just before the signing deadline. We
felt that Thomas had just edged ahead when it came down
to selection, for he was just that bit better in the air and
would be helpful to combat the aerial threat from David
Moss, the powerful attacker Alex Totten had bought from
Patrick Thistle who had done so well in the quarter-final
victory over St Johnstone at Brockville.

It has to be said that this was not one of our better
performances. We knew it would be important to settle
quickly and try to stamp our authority on the game. For all

that, we did get off to the best possible start with a fine goal from Stephane Adam, I hoped that would settle the side and that they would get full control of the match and start to dictate the flow and pace of the game. However, we just did not get going at all and we made too many basic mistakes in key areas which was not like us at all. We gave the ball away far too often and we let the First Division side in for a few chances but, it has to be said, they did not overwork Gilles Rousset in goal. Nevertheless, there is no point in beating about the bush – Falkirk were the better team in that opening 45 minutes.

Suffice to say that I was not a very happy manager as the players made their way to the dressing-room at the interval. I can't repeat the actual words that were used within the four walls of the dressing-room but some home truths were told in no uncertain terms. We had come through a first half in which we had played to an incredibly low standard, in a game that would take us through to the Cup final. We had allowed ourselves to be dominated by a team who were certainly up for the Cup challenge and the way we were going about our job was not acceptable to me or anyone else on the backroom staff. A few telling words were said privately to a couple of players here and there – and there was the problem that my former signing Kevin McAllister was causing us down the right wing. That had to be sorted out, and no one knew that better than Gary Naysmith who had just come through a difficult opening period. He had been given too much freedom but, fortunately, had not damaged us in terms of scoring goals. We had to get tighter to him to endeavour to influence the runs he was making from deep areas. However, credit has to be given where it is due and Kevin had a brilliant game that day – he was a handful for any defender to cope with, never mind a young kid playing in a Scottish Cup semi-final for the first time.

Much was made of Gary holding back a bit because he was only one booking away from missing the Scottish Cup final, but I told him that what mattered was getting to the Cup final. There was much criticism about Gary's performance in that final, but I thought the youngster handled himself exceptionally well. For all the work Falkirk had done in the tie, their non-stop battling and fighting tooth and nail to be first to the ball every time, I did not see them scoring at all in the second half. If they did, it was going to take something really exceptional to get them back on level terms. Our defence was coping quite well – Paul Ritchie and David Weir were in commanding form in the middle of the defence – but, to be perfectly honest, it was not going all that well for us in the middle of the park. We just could not get out of the bit, the quality was not there from the key area, which meant that our front three were not getting the usual supply of good service to stretch the opposing defence and add to that early goal. All too often the front men were left on their own without the necessary support.

Then came Kevin's goal, a break from the deep and a tremendous run and his shot from around the edge of the box gave Gilles absolutely no chance. It was a piece of outstanding individual magic, one of the finest goals ever scored. As I looked around the stadium, I could immediately sense the feeling amongst the Hearts fans. They must have had that sinking feeling and thought: 'Here we go again.' Five minutes of the game to go, and we were in danger of throwing it all away. I suppose many would have settled for a draw there and then, accept what we had, and live to fight another day in the hope that the team would then perform to their true capabilities. But that is neither the Jim Jefferies way nor the way I want my players to react in such a tense and difficult situation. It is in these situations that it is down to the players and how they react

151

to the upset. They can either fall apart at the seams or buckle down and show what they are made of. This was the time that we all saw what Hearts are all about. Our great strength is that we can score goals at any time in a game often out of nothing and at the time when the opposition is least expecting to be under attack. It was Wim Jansen who made that same point about us earlier in the season when he said that we scored goals when it really mattered. We could have fallen back into our defensive shell as Falkirk who, by this time had their tails up and wanted to come at us with all guns blazing and deliver the killer punch. Everyone sensed a Falkirk victory once they equalised, but it was at that very moment that Neil McCann came into his own and won the tie for Hearts. The move for our second goal was absolutely brilliant. In fact, we had looked a lot more composed and more authoritative when Lee Makel came into the game. It was Stephane Adam who started the move by coming deep and spraying the ball out to Neil who went on to take on the defence down the left-hand side. Neil, as we know, is a very quick player, but what was so impressive to us was the ground that Adam made up and he was there on the edge of the box to scoop McCann's cross into the roof of the net. Again, there was no sitting back – even when we saw that Falkirk were throwing everyone forward in a desperate bid to get back onto level terms, unfortunately, for Falkirk, that left gaps at the back. We realised that some of Falkirk's more experienced players started to feel the pace. This was seen when Neil Berry, a former great servant to the Hearts who had had a tremendous match, was left facing a one-on-one situation with Neil McCann after he broke from around the halfway line. There was going to be only one winner when it comes to pace but even then McCann still had a lot of work to do. He got away from the Falkirk defender and showed his composure and class with his calm finish to slot the ball across the body of the goalkeeper into the far corner of the net. That was a great feeling and how the Hearts fans reacted. It was as if the dark cloud of seeing the team stumble in cup competitions had been blown away and their reaction to the team was quite fantastic. It showed me that this team had grown in stature. They had matured together as a team, grown in character all season. They seem to be the kind of team that, when they jolted, respond – more often than not – in a very positive and determined fashion. The fans, I think, started to appreciate that here they had a team that could well go places. My words to the players in the dressing-room were quite short and simple: we had not played all that well for the 90 minutes but when questions had been asked of them, the response was there and we were in the Cup final.

To be perfectly frank, we had not played to a high standard in any of the early rounds of the Cup – and that includes the semi-finals – when we were up against lesser teams. However, the important thing, especially in cup football, is the result at the end of the day. There was nothing lucky about us making our way into the final but, to be fair, we made it without playing anywhere near our best. When I look back at the semi-final, to the opinions of the pundits and read all the headlines in the newspapers, all the attention was on Kevin's goal. I would be the last to take anything away from this great little footballer, and I have said his goal was right out of the top drawer, but the man who mattered above everyone else in that Ibrox tie was our own Neil McCann. He was the man for me, the player who did his bit to take his team through to the Cup final when the pressure was at its greatest.

Hearts had reached another Cup final – another opportunity for this new-look team to again knock at the door of trophy-winning success. Nothing comes easy in football, no one hands you anything on a plate, it has to be earned. It was an emotional time for me going in against my old team Falkirk on such a big occasion. It was at a time when Falkirk were fighting for their very existence, when the liquidators had been brought in and players that I had encouraged to come to Brockville were very worried about their future, and even concerned for a time if they were going to get paid. Too many people tend to forget that footballers are no different to any other professional – the same bills and the same mortgages have to be paid.

I felt for the club when it hit major financial trouble. I care about the club and I have made a financial contribution to the Save the Bairns fighting fund. It was something I felt I had to do and, until now, I have kept this very quiet. It was nobody else's business and the last thing I wanted to do is make this known at the time we were playing them in the Scottish Cup. There would have been some cynics, no doubt, who would have seen that as a ploy to try to seek some advantage.

I wanted to make sure that no one could ever accuse me of being party to any publicity trick. Anyone who knows me is very aware that that is not my style, never has been and never will be. I did it very quietly and privately. It is important that a club with the tradition of Falkirk survives – we need clubs like that in the Scottish game. As in any walk of life, it only really comes home to you when you are involved in the club in some way or another and I certainly was involved in the Falkirk set-up for a good few years. It was no easy ride when I was there, there was a terrible shortage of money and I had to wheel and deal all the time to have any chance of bringing in new players. I was aware of the problems behind the scenes, a lot of in-fighting in the boardroom, but Billy and I kept well away from any involvement. All we were looking at was putting the best possible Falkirk team on the park and giving the fans something to shout about. It was a hard struggle and I must say that a lot of credit must go to Campbell Christie, the former general secretary of the Scottish Trades Union Congress. He took over as chairman, the local man, and he held things together when it was getting really difficult with so much bickering going on. He was a very nice man who had a great feeling for Falkirk, his local football team. I got on with my job, just as I do with Hearts, but at least the money they earned from their Cup run helped keep their heads above water and saw them through to the end of the season before further changes were made. Now a new group has taken over the running of the club. The Falkirk scenario shows just how difficult life can be in running a football club. It was not easy for a while at Hearts when Leslie Deans and Chris Robinson took over from Wallace Mercer; they had a massive job on their hands and it is remarkable to see what has been achieved off the field in the last few years. It fills me with pride to look at Tynecastle these days, to see those three new stands, all the new corporate facilities and other improvements to give the Hearts fans a ground to be proud of. However, the success of any football club, no matter what anyone might think, is judged by what happens on the park . . . and there was still much to do at Tynecastle in the weeks before the Scottish Cup final.

It was Rangers again – three Cup finals in three seasons for me and every time it was Walter Smith and his star-studded side that had to be overcome. It was looking all the time, as eventually proved to be the case, that the Scottish Cup would be the one and only chance to win a trophy and it was Walter Smith's last game in charge. Rangers had not finished a season for 12 years without a domestic trophy and Hearts stood between them and a barren season. I had gone to the semi-final against Celtic – which had been played at Celtic Park – and Walter's side came out on top on the night and it was an impressive performance. Before that tie, 24 hours after we had beaten Falkirk at Ibrox, people kept on asking me which one of the Old Firm teams I would prefer to meet in the final. It did not really matter, we had played each of them four times in the league and had never managed a single win. This so-called failure against the two big Glasgow clubs had been thrown at me and my players all season so we had something to prove, no matter who our opponents were. Our own league campaign had faltered immediately after the semi-final and the big turning point for us was our failure to beat Motherwell in front of our own fans on an awful night at Tynecastle. It was touch and go if the game would go on, but it did, we managed to get our noses in front then we just stopped doing what we are good at. It is not the Hearts way to sit back; we are not very good at it, but footballers are only human and, no doubt, they thought they would try to hold on to what they had and we were punished. The game ended in a draw and I knew there and then that it was the end of our great challenge for the league title. It was a real downer but we had to pick ourselves up.

What was critical was that we had to respond, particularly after the three-goal defeat at the hands of Rangers in the final league meeting, in what had been looked upon as the Scottish Cup final dress-rehearsal. It was not a good day and right after the game the players were told to be at Tynecastle first thing on Sunday morning. Not a lot more was said and, no doubt, they spent that Saturday night feeling they were about to get a right roasting from me and Billy. I was not happy with their attitude, it was not acceptable to me and not good enough for Heart of Midlothian Football Club. I suppose they were expecting a tongue-lashing and then a hammering on the training ground. What happened was the exact opposite. We sat down as a group in the dressing-room, talked things through, I made my points about what had gone wrong, told a few home truths here and there and demanded a better response, and then we went out on the pitch for nothing more than a very light training session. There are ways and means to get the message over. After all, these were the very same players who had performed so superbly all season and had deservedly won a lot of praise for their efforts and applications. However, standards have to be maintained from the start of the season to the finish and we really needed to get back to playing something like our old selves in the few remaining games, and I really took heart from our performance at Aberdeen.

Colin Cameron had been out of the team for a while, told to take a complete rest in a bid to get him back into action and ready to give his all in the Cup final. The plan was to give him a game at Pittodrie and then let him have a rest against Dunfermline and then get involved in the intense preparations for the final. We did quite well in that game but, in the last game of the season, we played extremely well were right back to the form that we had shown earlier in the season, which had seen us at the top of the league for a while and playing some outstanding football and scoring a lot of goals into the bargain. That really pleased me, we were given a standing ovation by the fans, which was a great send-off.

All thoughts were on the final and we decided to take a completely different approach, head out of Scotland and prepare in the Midlands at the beautiful Stratford-upon-Avon. We had been to Durham a couple of times, perfectly good and adequate facilities, but that had been our base for the previous Scottish Cup final against Rangers and we had suffered a terrible 5–1 hammering. This time everything was just right. The team bus left Tynecastle on the Saturday night with all our gear and headed south; while we had to fly to London – simply because we could not all get on a direct flight to Birmingham. The team bus was there to meet us at Heathrow and that was the start of the preparations for the big bid to make the trophy-winning breakthrough. All teams go away at some stage to prepare for a major game, be it a big European tie or a major cup final. It is essential to find an environment where players can be completely focused on the job in hand without any outside interference. Since we had beaten Falkirk, cup fever had gripped Gorgie, the euphoria was growing for weeks with our supporters so keen for us to do well, with the hunt for tickets to be at Celtic Park for that remarkable May day was in full swing. Players just have to get away from that and that is what we did. Stratford was a new base for us and it was brilliant. The Scotland squad had used the very same facilities as us at the National Farmers' Union headquarters and Craig Brown strongly recommended the set-up to me as the perfect base . . . and how right he was. We could not have wished for any better; the facilities there are as good as you will find anywhere. We used the Forest of Arden as our base and we started in a very relaxed fashion – the players had the Sunday night to themselves and some of them opted for a game of golf, and I played a few holes myself, sore back and all. It was part of the plan to get the players into the right frame of mind straight from the very start, in what was a thoroughly organised week from start to finish.

We had a squad of 20 players with us – skipper Gary Locke had been left at home to have intensive treatment in the hope of being fit – and very early on we sat them down together, gave them details on the bonus that was on offer for winning the Cup and explained that everyone, whether they started, were on the bench, or were six of the unlucky ones who would not be involved and would have to sit and watch the final from the stand, would get a share of the bonus. No one was being left out. That is the way it has to be done in my book. Football these days is very much a squad game, it is not all about 11 or 14 men, it is all about the pool of players who can step into the first team whenever they are required and can turn in the high level of performance that is expected from them. This is not the time when you leave players out in the cold one minute and then ask them to deliver for you at the drop of a hat. For me, at any rate, that is the only way to run the playing side.

But right from that first minute when we gathered on the Sunday morning at Edinburgh airport the message started to be hammered home that this was our time, the great chance to bring the Cup back to Edinburgh. We were aware that one of the big Rangers players, Jorg Albertz, would miss the final because of SFA suspension and that would be an obvious handicap to Rangers for he was such an influential player for them and was at the top of his form. We had found that out to our cost earlier in the season as we suffered from his lethal finishing and, at that time, he was having one of his best-ever spells in a Rangers jersey. On top of that Paul Gascoigne had left Ibrox to head for Middlesbrough in a deal worth more than £4 million. No matter what anyone says about Gazza and what he did off the field, there can never be any doubt that he was a hugely influential player on the field and had done a great job for Rangers. He had won the Player of the Year award and that was totally deserved. Laudrup was the one man we had to keep very quiet – even though I didn't feel he was at the top of his form – as we felt that, when it came to inflicting serious damage on us, we had no need to fear any other player in the Rangers team. But right from the start of Cup-final week, it was all about how Hearts played – and the very style we adopted to meet the demands of this one massive game for both clubs.

We kept on trying to convince the boys that there was no point in going to Celtic Park for the final if they did not have that inner belief, the confidence, to win the trophy. As I have kept on saying, we had not beaten Rangers all season and it was clear to me and Billy it was all down to the way we played against them. We had won a lot of plaudits all season, three players up all the time and having a go at the opposition from start to finish. It brought us a lot of rewards, the fans loved the attacking style and the number of goals that we had scored – and we had gone to places like Kilmarnock and Motherwell and flattened the opposition with a goal rush. That was fine, but not good enough against Rangers. The way we played suited them perfectly as they like nothing better than the team coming at them and then striking hard and fast on the break with some lethal finishing. There's no one better at doing that than Laudrup, often with great support from Gordon Durie. They simply rip the opposition apart in a two against two situation or even three against two. They are just so quick and highly skilled and, when given the space, they will punish you and very few teams come back from that.

All that week we worked on a new system, playing Rangers virtually at their own game by playing one up. We had the privacy we needed to work twice a day on the system but the one little problem was that McCann, a key man to the system, had a niggling minor injury that kept him out of the system. The game plan against Rangers was to play one up with Laudrup playing off him, but if we played just one up we would have more men in other areas to stifle their attacking forays and then look to hit them on the counter-attack. In certain areas, we wanted to give Rangers more of the ball than they usually expect against us.

It meant asking some players to take on different roles and we used some of our own players, like Jim Hamilton and José Quitongo, to take on the role of the Rangers players to see how our own players would react. It was not a thing you could labour on for too long, but I felt we did enough to give everyone the feel of it. We kept on changing things around a bit here and there to keep the players on their toes as to the starting line-up, but as the week wore on they started to grasp the overall picture. We knew it would not be perfect by any manner of means.

Overall, the few days away were a great success and the finest tribute I can pay to the people down at Stratford, and particularly the NFU, is that they helped in our bid to win the Cup. They just could not do enough for us. Everything we could have wished for was provided – it was five-star service all the way. The training pitches could not have been better, a special conference room was laid aside for us to have our meetings in whenever we wanted. There was not a single worry all week and I must say a personal thank you to the NFU chief executive, Andrew Young. He's a great Rangers supporter, a season-ticket-holder, but he was never far away from us and was always on hand to make sure we had everything we needed. He even came to have his picture taken with us – though I can't remember if he was wearing his Rangers scarf or not. We invited him to be our guest at the final but he was out of the country at the time on business – and maybe that was just as well. When we left there on the Wednesday we knew we would never be better prepared to give of our best, but there was still a little concern over the team selection. I knew that McCann would be all right for action but there was a worry about Colin Cameron. He had had a cortisone injection at the start of the week to ease his pelvic problem, but the closer the Saturday came, the more I knew he would make it – although he did need another localised injection before the final. It then comes down to the manager to pick the team for the job in hand and one of the biggest selection problems surrounded Jim Hamilton. He had been such a great player for us during the season but had been forced to miss the last three league games because of SFA suspension. He had scored twice against Rangers earlier in the season and he was also good in defensive areas. The bottom line was that to have played Jim from the start would have meant changing our system. He is a different type of player to Stephane Adam and the way I wanted to play meant having John Robertson, Jim Hamilton and Grant Murray on the bench when the ideal set-up would have been to have a defender, a midfield man and forward held back in reserve on the substitutes bench. However, I felt that with so many midfield players in the starting line-up I could afford to go with two forwards on the bench. A lot of people expected me to play Grant at right-back but I decided to go with Davie McPherson, mainly for his experience plus his strength in the air during set pieces in both attacking and defensive situations.

The actual team was named to the players on the Friday afternoon before we headed to Dunblane Hydro on the eve of the final. The boys had been out on the park loosening up when we called them into the dressing-room and got down to the business in hand. We had a general team talk, going over what had been done all week, and then let everyone know who was in the team, with the naming of the substitutes held back to the Saturday morning.

We had 20 players in the dressing-room, along with Gary Locke who I decided to take with us to the hotel. Again I kept on telling them that we were all in this together, every single one of us, and we were all going to share the glory. This was Hearts – no individuals, but every single person at the club all pulling together. This was their chance of glory and the incentives, if needed, were there in terms of a financial reward which was substantial. When the team was named, the response from those who were left out was as I anticipated: to a man they were so supportive and right behind everyone.

It was quite a night in Dunblane, the players were in bed early after a meal, while the backroom staff spent some time sitting in the hotel ballroom chatting away as old-time dancing went on around us, accompanied by the music of Jim MacLeod and his band. We had plenty of hotel residents coming forward to wish us all the best in the final and that was much appreciated. The morning of the final I sensed we were all up for it and I was convinced we were going to win. I kept on telling the team, either collectively or individually, that here was the chance to have the greatest day of our footballing lives. During the build-up, much was made about the 42-year wait and understandably so. There was Freddie Glidden, John Cumming and Bobby Kirk all being paraded again as the heroes of the 1956 Cup-winning side. Every one of them was a Hearts great, but I kept on telling the players that here was their chance to become legends, the fans would start to talk about the McCanns, the Fultons, the Hamiltons, the Weirs and the Robertsons in the very same breath as the former heroes. This was their big chance to be Hearts greats. It was non-stop talk about winning and telling them that they could never ever imagine the reception they would receive from the people of Edinburgh if that famous trophy was brought back to Tynecastle. There were so many thousands of fans who had never seen that trophy in Edinburgh and it was time to get all that frustration buried once and for all – get the monkey off the back of the club that had been there for so many years.

We were the first team to arrive at Celtic Park and the welcome we had from our fans was incredible – they were willing us to win the trophy and, again, that message of winning was all the talk of the dressing-room up to the very second that the team emerged into the sunshine and the noise that greeted them from the stadium was incredible. Playing in a final is all about getting off to a good start and, for all the planning and scheming during the week, you never know what is going to happen when that whistle blows. For us it was incredible – just a few seconds on the clock and referee Willie Young was pointing to the penalty spot. I must say that when the referee pointed to the spot I just happened to look at the bench and sitting there was John Robertson, a great penalty-kick taker. 'Maybe I should have started with him', was the thought that flashed through my mind. But Colin was the man. What a difficult situation for him against Andy Goram, a great goalkeeper who has bailed out Rangers in many such moments down through the years. I have to confess I thought about not watching but, no, I had to stay focused and I turned my gaze on Colin. What a penalty, a superb strike into the back of the net. For some reason or other I turned round and saw Chick Young of BBC Scotland sitting right behind the dugout and asked him, 'How long to go?'

There has been much made about penalty-kicks since then, with all the controversy at the World Cup finals of nations going out in a penalty shoot-out, like England who suffered when David Batty missed against Argentina. At Tynecastle, our lads often have a penalty-kick contest after training with either Gilles Rousset or Roddy McKenzie in goal. It is something I encourage, as it creates a lot of banter between the lads and further boosts team spirit.

That penalty gave us the dream start and it put the onus on Rangers. We just had to keep things tight and then go for the second goal. The only thing we did wrong in the first half was that we sat a bit too deep at times – but that is a natural reaction. However, it was important for us to take the initiative again, to stamp our authority on the game and we had to encourage Flogel and McCann to be a bit more positive. The words in the dressing-room at the break were all about encouragement; we were going well but still had to look to go forward looking for the second goal. As expected, Ally McCoist appeared on the scene for Rangers and they did give us a couple of scares, but I knew we could get a chance and if we did we had to take it. It came through an act of great opportunism from Adam as he caught Lorenzo Amoruso napping and, before Amoruso had recovered, Adam had nicked ahead of him and beaten Andy Goram with a cracking shot. I knew it was in straight away for McCann's hands went up immediately, and credit also goes to Neil; he had followed up well if Andy had kept it out, so that the wee man would have knocked home the rebound for sure. We could have had a third when Flogel had a great chance, but his power header went straight at Goram. If it had gone away from him it would have ended in the back of the neck.

It was now the countdown to glory and I had just turned to Billy to say that if we could hold it at 2–0 with just minutes to go, then the Cup would be ours. I had just got the words out of my mouth when Ally scored. It was the longest few minutes of my life but I looked at my players and I saw the determination of them and knew they could do it. Jim Hamilton had come on and he won some magnificent balls in the air when the pressure was on during that nightmare last few minutes. David Weir made some great tackles, Paul Ritchie was immense for one so young, and there was that awful moment when Ally went down and Rangers screamed for a penalty. I turned to Walter and he said it was a penalty, but then my eye caught Willie Young. He had darted forward and looked at his linesman and when I saw

165

the linesman, stood his ground and had not made the dash to the corner flag – which he would have done if it had been a penalty – I was very relieved. Everyone on our bench was praying for Amoruso to take the free-kick – he had taken them all afternoon and, fortunately for us, he had left his shooting boots at home. Up stepped Brian Laudrup and that was what I feared – this time he did not execute it too well. It was a terrible time, I could sense the tension of the Hearts fans and I must say I clenched my fists when Gordon Durie burst into the box. It was the last chance and when the ball flew over the bar I knew then that the Cup was ours.

Words just cannot describe my feelings when the whistle blew – the dream had come true and it was hard for me to think that here I was, the Hearts fan from Wallyford, who had brought the Cup back to Tynecastle. My dad Jimmy was there to savour the moment – but not my mother. Earlier in the week my dad had come to me to hand back a ticket I had for the family and I thought something was wrong. My dad suggested I should go to the house after training and there was my mum telling me she was not going to the final. She could not; it was the annual guild outing and so she was off to Falkirk and Calendar Park. She had been going there for 20 years and no way was she missing the outing with her friends. Maybe she did not want to be at the stadium because of the tension – but it meant as much to her as the 20,000 fans at Celtic Park to see the trophy being won. As the place went mad I was hustled up the tunnel to do an immediate media interview and, for the first time in my life, I choked. I thought I could handle it all, but not this time; the words would just not come out and I just remember standing there with Neil Pointon and some of the other lads nearby and I just kept saying 'Yes! Yes!'. In retrospect maybe it was just as well, for I was back on an even keel as I came out onto the pitch to join in the celebrations with the lads.

From then on it was celebrations all the way – Robbo's dream had come true – and we all just could not wait to get back to Edinburgh for what was to be a never-to-be-forgotten 24 hours – we were all on an incredible high, drunk on adrenalin. The return to Tynecastle was everything I had dreamt of – and much, much more. Tears of joy and triumph were in abundance as we were met by a police Land Rover to escort us into the city. There it was, bedecked in maroon and white and I believe that the policemen had volunteered to do the job for nothing because they were great Hearts fans. The nearer we came to the city the more the expectation grew, and I will always remember the sight of coming near the fire station at Sighthill and all the fire engines were on parade at the side of the road with the firemen cheering us. The crowds grew and grew with every passing yard, with Gary Locke at the front of the bus holding the Scottish Cup in an iron-like grip. There was no way he would let it go and as we hit Gorgie and turned into Tynecastle for our reception, some of the players, unknown to me, were on the roof of the bus to wave to the masses of supporters. Mums, dads, grannies and granddads were all out on the streets as we slowly made our way into the stadium and a reception in the new corporate area, an absolutely fabulous night. I thought nothing could match that homecoming – but the official reception was still to come and the Sunday parade through the streets.

Early on Sunday morning I left the Caledonian Hotel with a few friends for a breath of air and our stroll took us along Shandwick Place, a visit to the chemist was high on the agenda. The streets were deserted until as we turned the corner, there, coming towards me, was a quite elderly-looking man bedecked in maroon but his head was down, no doubt returning from his own celebrations. The head never came up and as he passed I said to him: 'Did you enjoy our day?' He never broke stride and muttered: 'Oh, what a fabulous day – see that Jim Jefferies, God bless him!' On he walked, I looked at my friends and burst out laughing. I am sure that when he turned the corner he would say to himself; 'Wait a minute, was that Jim Jefferies? No, it couldn't be – I must be dreaming. I've had a big night out – I'm still drunk.' Let me assure him he was not dreaming; it was Jim Jefferies he was talking to. And if he reads this then I would welcome a call from him and he can come to Tynecastle to see the Cup.

For the rest of the Sunday the streets were packed and the open-top bus journey from the City Chambers, which Lord Provost Eric Milligan joined, was just incredible. Everywhere you turned the streets were a sea of maroon. As we hit Princes Street I looked behind the bus and all you could see was a sea of people; every vantage point was utilised and we even had the Hearts version of *The Full Monty* from a group of lads on a rooftop. I felt the bus would never get along Gorgie because there were so many people there and we still had to hit Tynecastle where the ground was bursting at the seams. The Hearts fans had come to celebrate – the party was in full swing but my day was far from finished.

Later, it was back to Glasgow to pick up the Manager of the Year award at the Scottish Football Writers' Association dinner – an honour I thought was sure to go to Wim Jansen for his great achievement in winning the league championship in his first season at Celtic Park. In fact, it had been before the Cup final when it was first announced that I had won the award and the thought did cross my mind that I might win this accolade and yet not win a trophy. However, I knew that the award was in recognition of what Hearts had achieved, not me, in competing so

strongly for the league championship with so few resources. Some people did ask me when I arrived at the
dinner why I had not brought the Scottish Cup with me.
How could I, was my quick reaction, we had waited 42
years to bring the Cup to Edinburgh and it was certainly
not leaving the city again within 24 hours. I felt very
privileged to have won the award, but it was an award for
everyone at Hearts.

It has been a great year for the club, so much has been
done in such a short space of time and we have brought a
lot of joy and happiness to thousands of Hearts supporters.
However, I have to accept that now we have climbed a rung
higher in the ladder of expectation. The job does not end
because we have won the Scottish Cup . . . it is really only
starting as far as I am concerned. We have all enjoyed every
second of that magical day in May but now it has to be put
on the back-burner. It is all about going forward. The
Scottish Cup has to be looked upon as a platform, proof that
that club can be winners again and we have to give it all we
can to continue the success story. No one is going to say
that that is an easy objective to achieve, but that is what we
have to aim for. There is no time in football to stand still,
particularly when a top honour has been won. The players
have now had a taste of success and have proved to
everyone that they are capable of being acclaimed winners.
We have to try to do it all again and the players have
already been told that.

One of the first things we did after the players reported
back to Tynecastle, at the start of pre-season training early
in July, was to tell them that it was back to square one – we
have to start all over again and try to bring more success. It
is easy to say that but, without question, it is getting more
difficult with every passing season. It was hard to compete
against the likes of Rangers and Celtic in the 1980s, but

Aberdeen and Dundee United did it and that was a fabulous achievement for them. The record books show it is even more difficult in the 1990s, as the success of Rangers has proved, dominating the league championship scene all the way through until Celtic ended their great run to deny them that record tenth title in a row. Towards the millennium it will get tougher because the Old Firm, with every passing season, are on a different plane when it comes to buying players.

Rangers have a new coach in Dick Advocaat, the first foreigner to manage the Ibrox club in their 125-year history, and within the first two weeks of moving in as the successor to Walter Smith he splashed out a massive £14 million on new players – most of them World Cup stars – including the top Dutch defender Arthur Numan. This is what we are competing against in what is a new era for Scottish football and a very exciting one. We know we have to keep Hearts right up there with the very best and it is going to take a massive effort from everyone. Other teams will be looking to make their mark. Look at Aberdeen, they have made a massive investment up at Pittodrie in an all-out bid to bring success back to the north-east.

What we have at Hearts is a fresh beginning with a comparatively young side, who I believe have still to reach their peak as individuals. It has been a huge boost to have been able to persuade so many of the players to agree to new or long-term extensions to their present contracts which gives us a very important degree of stability. We have a good nucleus, the strongest squad that has been at this club for many a long year, but my job is to continue to strive to seek further and long-lasting improvements. It takes total commitment from all concerned but I am totally convinced we are on the right road to ensuring that Hearts stay up there as a major force, and there is no doubt that a terrific support helps. When I first came to Tynecastle there were hardly 3,000 season-ticket-holders. That figure has been steadily increasing over the last couple of years and, following our Scottish Cup win, we now have almost 14,000 fans who have bought season-tickets for the challenge ahead. That indicates to me that they like what they are seeing. Having a packed Tynecastle for every home game is a massive bonus. But we have to keep on delivering. But in May 1998, as the song goes, 'The talk of the toon are the boys in maroon' – a year never to be forgotten in the history of this great club and the proudest moment of my footballing career – so far!